MW01279945

THE SOCIAL MEDIA SURVIVAL GUIDE

Everything You Need to Know to Grow Your
Business Exponentially with Social Media

Sherrie A. Madia, Ph.D.
Paul Borgese

Full Court Press

Full Court Press
A Division of Base Camp Communications, LLC
3 Woodstone Drive
Voorhees, NJ 08043

Find Us Online:
SocialMediaSurvivalGuide.com

Library of Congress Cataloging-in-Publication Data
Madia, Sherrie Ann, and Borgese, Paul.
The Social Media Survival Guide / by Sherrie Madia and Paul Borgese.

Summary: Best practices for implementing sustainable social media strategies for business success.
  p. cm.

ISBN: 978-0-9826185-1-6

2010920310

Printed in the United States of America

10 9 8 7 6 5 4 3 2 1 Second Edition

There's something happening here
What it is ain't exactly clear
There's a man with a gun over there
Telling me I got to beware
I think it's time we stop, children, what's that sound
Everybody look what's going down

—Buffalo Springfield from the song "For What It's Worth"

CONTENTS

PART III: Bring It

SURVIVAL KITS

ACKNOWLEDGMENTS

A S WITH ANY PROJECT THAT EVOLVES as the content itself evolves, this book would not have come to fruition without the help of a team of dedicated individuals. Special thanks go to Dominique Basile, who worked tirelessly in between her efforts to earn her MBA from the Wharton School; Eric Herr, longtime business writer and broadcast professional; Allison Katz, for her ability to encapsulate complex applications into bite-sized pieces; Liza Lozovatskaya, for her diligence in research; Kathy Shaidle, whose passion for social media is apparent and ongoing (no more articles, please—we have to go to press!) and Sonja Sherwood, who helped capture the essentials of how businesses are approaching social media. All demonstrated outstanding research efforts, and a keen ability to hunt down up-to-the-minute research on all things social media. The team worked under tight deadlines and produced the highest-quality results. And thanks to Julee Song for her smart cover design. Any oversights in this text are clearly ours, though we can't be held responsible for any applications mentioned that have since evolved or devolved, as such is the state of social media. That said, we hope to have provided not only the most stable applications, but more importantly, the most stable approaches to using social media tactics in ways that are well thought out and applicable regardless of which new application appears on the scene. If you're new to the social media space, we are thankful that you are giving this book a read, as our hope is that this will become the first step in demystifying social media, and optimizing tactics to ensure your organization's ultimate advantage in the marketplace.

WHY READ THIS BOOK?

AS WE SET FORTH TO WRITE THIS BOOK, we realized something important: Not only is the sea of social media vast, but the sea of social media books is keeping pace. You might read all day, every day, and find that you still aren't clear on what it's all about.

We don't think this is a good use of your time.

And we don't think becoming a technical expert in search-engine marketing keywords or programming in CSS for your Twitter page makes much sense either. That's what your IT and creative teams are there to do.

We do think that if you are able to acquire an understanding of the strategy implications surrounding social media, and envision these as elements to integrate within your current marketing and communications plan, you'll gain back all the time you'll need to focus on planning and execution. You can make an immediate impact on your efforts to engage core targets and emerge a hero in your corporation not for facilitating social media, but for facilitating *smart* social media.

ONE LUMP OR TWO?

If you haven't yet activated a social media strategy within your organization, you may think everyone has long since bought into the social media craze and you're the last great holdout. You may then be surprised to learn that more companies than not are still unclear about what they should be doing in this digital space—and for some, even whether they want to get involved at all.

Organizations are finding themselves challenged in ways they haven't before had to consider. Problems such as declining memberships, subscriptions, and product sales, and the loss of what may have been considered "regulars" in their customer base are just some of what's keeping most professionals charged with growing their company's bottom line up at night.

In the wake of easy access to products just like yours (only at discounted prices) or networking through social media sites (saves that annual $299 membership fee!), not to mention industry knowledge now gleaned through webinars, podcasts and video tutorials—the glut of them offered for free—many of the foregone conclusions we may have drawn in the past about consumers' appetites for our insights, skills and great products are simply no longer accurate.

And the state of the economy has only served to exacerbate this dilemma.

Now more than ever, longstanding and upstart organizations, big brands and mom-and-pop shops across all industries—every last one—must offer tangible, tactical value to consumers...or risk losing them completely.

And yet, these organizations—your organization—is also in a unique position to ramp up the engagement with target groups by establishing core social media elements designed to arm consumers with value-added solutions to their most pressing needs.

To state the opportunity clearly: If you're feeling like your brand is passé, or your organization is "out of it" when it comes to tapping into consumers and growing profit, **social media is your chance to be relevant again.**

From not-for-profits to organizations and associations in government and the corporate sector, the needs are the same: Consumers who like your brand want the inside track and the value-adds. Consumers who don't like your brand also need to be part of your inner circle because this will enable you to better understand their concerns, and address them—before they topple you.

Even one sour note in the Twittersphere can launch a public relations disaster for your brand. We've seen this too often from brands who simply didn't know what they didn't know.

And trust us, the energy you'll spend on containing these disasters—if containment is even possible—is generally far more intensive than the time it would have taken to do things right in the first place. But this means knowing where to start.

Thus, our goal is to help you to ramp up fast and start applying social networking tactics as a means of not only avoiding major crises, but also—and more importantly—driving sales, meeting and beating the competition, and developing ways to implement essential tools designed to create immediate engagement with audiences. If social networking is properly executed, you will see dramatic bottom-line results.

If you're wondering why your tried-and-true strategies are no longer working, it's likely not because you've taken your eye off the ball, but rather because your customer base is now playing a different game on a different field.

If you're looking to regain lost sales and profits, or grow your already viable consumer base, you must create new channels of information that address the needs of your target groups not once, but on an ongoing, sustainable basis. From a stakeholder and a shareholder perspective, gone are the days of the once-a-year mega-sale, or the quarterly update with silence during the months in between—each with its limited scope and opportunity.

Today's consumer appetite calls for all-the-time, anytime engagement, which, depending on your resources, may translate into a monthly, weekly, or daily basis. Don't believe us? Check out your competition, or business models similar to yours. Are your competitors sending daily updates to consumers on their cell phones?

If the answer is yes, then they're beating you.

Perhaps not on a product-to-product basis, but they're beating you at being top-of-mind in the consumer's head, compared to your occasional push of information.

Want to change all that? The first step is getting to know your customers. This is followed closely by the need to let your customers get to know you.

And this is where *The Social Media Survival Guide* will help by offering practical advice on best practices, pitfalls to avoid within the context of traditional marketing (e.g., targeting and position-ing), tactics, resources and the corporate buy-in you'll need to succeed.

We'll take you from tactical considerations through strategic planning and help you to develop your knowledge of the real skills you will need to use and oversee social media tools.

The information provided here is offered from the perspective of marketing and corporate communications, and is designed to help you to assess the level of technical skill required to launch social media applications within your organization—and maintain them successfully. If you are a professional who needs to understand, use and make decisions about social media, then this book is for you.

Each chapter will focus on practical knowledge—including knowing what each tool can do for your brand, which tools to choose, how to manage resources effectively and realistically, and how to employ diligence in listening, testing and measuring results along the way.

We'll guide you through strategic use of applications such as Twitter, Facebook, YouTube and more, and will offer important insights into social media policy and staffing that you'll need to consider, as well as the new dilemma that many companies are beginning to face, from the C-Suite to the mailroom, of striking a balance between personal and professional identity.

Ramping up with social media applications doesn't need to be arduous. This book will help you to navigate with tips and tactics to construct value-added social media applications, while honing in on the skills you already possess.

Social media is all about creating an ongoing conversation with your target groups, so we'll present best practices for the ideal types of conversations you'll need to create and maintain.

Finally, we'll offer a surefire approach to combining social media seamlessly and effectively within your existing marketing and communications plan. Our goal is that when you've finished this book you will be armed to address one core goal through social media tactics: **affecting positive return on investment**.

The Social Media Survival Guide, now in its second edition, will take you through such vital elements as:

- Assessing corporate buy-in: Your success in social media will be determined by the organizational base of support

- Determining broad-based objectives to minimize risk and maximize opportunity

- Understanding your organization's skill set to determine what you know and what you need to know about social media applications

- Tips for calling in the experts: Signs to look for when engaging an expert—and how to ensure that an expert is what you're really getting

- Developing a mini social media campaign: This doesn't mean setting up a Facebook account and walking away, but rather, devising a manageable exercise designed to enable your organization to test the waters first before jumping in completely

- Understanding the value proposition that social media provides and harnessing this to enhance your existing effort

- Setting the groundwork for next-generation solutions to ensure ongoing success in the social media space as a standard part of planning and implementation

PART I

Who Moved My Audience?

DON'T BE ALARMED, but in the midst of all of the excitement over Web 2.0 and new media, there's something you should know: The significance of social media as a whole lies somewhere between the Pet Rock and the printing press. That is, some elements will trend and fade, while others will cause—and have already caused—significant and irreversible change in consumer behavior, and thus, in corporate response and positioning.

1

Déjà vu All Over Again...Again

THE ABOVE SENTIMENT might seem a bit hard to swallow, particularly if you've been charged with utilizing social media to keep your company relevant in the current new media space. Regardless of which elements of the Web 2.0 platform and social media tactics are here to stay, the dynamics of engagement have shifted the paradigm in ways that no one can afford to ignore. This paradigm shift has left many marketing and communications professionals reeling, whether they'll admit it or not.

But much of new media isn't really new at all. Our business objectives are largely the same, we are still trying hard to engage audiences in our brands and our products, and we seek to optimize positive publicity and minimize the crises. In the midst of scrambling to meet these objectives through social networking tactics, you may have noticed that there is an almost disturbing number of "social media experts" in the online space.

In a sense, it's almost not their fault for thinking they know more than they do. Today, anybody can be a publisher, a writer, a journalist—why not a social media professional? After all, if I'm a voracious blogger, doesn't that make me an expert? Not exactly. There is a massive divide between being a user of social media and possessing a thorough knowledge of its strategic applications. More often than not, companies are confusing use with knowledge.

In part, this is due to its origins. Let's take a quick detour down the path of social media history. We won't have to walk far. The history of the most stable of social media applications that are causing a stir stretches back only as far as a handful of years—to 2004 to be exact. Just six years ago, we couldn't have delivered this book to you because the technology wouldn't have been here, and the applications wouldn't have been derived, and the paradigm shift in how we communicate and consume information would not yet have been in place.

While the waters aren't overly deep when we are searching for historical significance, the rapid iterations in the online space have enabled a massive collection of data from which to draw best practices.

Amidst the speed of technological advancements, next-generation functionality churns out on a daily basis. This fast and furious pace is part of what drives users to misuses and abuses of some powerful applications.

The landscape that marketing professionals—and by this, we include marketing, advertising, public relations and corporate communications professionals—has dramatically changed, and it's an evolution that happened with stunning speed (read "Stone Age to Industrial Revolution" in a half-dozen years).

Now more than any other time in the corporate and non-profit sectors across the globe, the general workforce needs to care about marketing and communications best practices.

How so? Because the lines between back office, behind-the-scenes workforce and customer-facing staff have blurred. On Delta Airlines' corporate blog, for example, we might hear from "Judy" in IT, sharing a new technology designed to make checking a bag faster for you—and you are thus invited to ask her a question about this new upgrade. That wouldn't have been an option even a few years back. And it opens your brand to both opportunity and risk.

Because of this, corporate responses to social media have varied dramatically: "Ignore it." "Reject it." "Embrace it." We'll unpack these responses as we offer recommendations for confronting social media, understanding what it can and cannot do for your organization, and developing a tactical plan designed to get you into the space successfully, while measuring return against your marketing dollars.

As a marketing and communications professional, your initial reaction to social media may have gone something like this: You might have thought closing all the blinds might help. You may have tried laughing it off as just another fad—or shutting your mouth tight and refusing to try it. You may have kicked or screamed or pitched a fit. And yet, there it stood—solid and fastidious, like an icy plate of food on meatloaf night—risk and opportunity rolled up into one: this thing called social media..

If you've been listening to the atmosphere far more than you have been tuned in to hasty recommendations that companies must rush to overpopulate the blogosphere or tweet until they're hoarse without just cause, you're not alone. But if you've been cautious to adapt and adopt—or are intrigued but uncertain as to how to make a go of it—you must now begin to test core tactics, and then apply the learnings and mainstream elements into your marketing and communications plans. From our work with clients across industries, we know that the later you arrive at the party, the more reluctant you may be to enter at all, but consider that much has been tested—and discarded and revised—as you've warmed the bench, so this just makes your job easier.

Unlike other major technological innovations (e.g., the World Wide Web), which were reserved for IT groups and thus, exempted the rest of the organization, with social media—designed to engage all users—assumptions are likely to be made. You may not know Twitter from the telephone, but if you are charged with overseeing marketing, communications, or public relations within your organization, the perception may be that you are the one with the answers. And you'll likely be asked to engage in different ways with the publics you encounter via social media applications. But being a user of social media and understanding the strategy behind effective use of core tactics are two dramatically different skill sets.

What we're seeing today is that organizations are not necessarily making these distinctions, and while great things are happening, in like quantity, mistakes are being made.

Whereas several years back, those creating messages and communicating through tried distribution channels knew their craft inside and out, in many ways, social media snuck up behind them, infiltrated their consumers' information habits, and made solid professionals feel as though their years of experience in the trenches had become obsolete.

That said, if you've been honing your skills in marketing, communications and public relations, then you are brilliantly positioned for social media tactics—far and away beyond those who have entered through an IT door, or on the coattails of a social media application. In fact, with just a little bit of knowledge, you will begin to see the powerful tools that are at your disposal.

Many companies think they have two choices: take a polar bear dive into icy waters, or simply stagnate on the shore. If you are a marketer, or a businessperson struggling with how to spend resources effectively, and you've been harboring a secret skepticism about some of the new tactics that have presented themselves, good for you. After all, aren't we all trained to ask questions, to reason things out, and to tread cautiously until we're fully up to speed on cost and value and resources and return?

If you bring with you even an ounce of feeling slightly out of it in your role as a marketer, communicator, or public relations professional, now's the time to put that feeling aside, and to reassure yourself that the reason you've probably balked or hesitated from the start is that, as you've likely done your whole career, you know better than to run fast at every shiny object.

Granted, with the onslaught of new social media tools available, the task of determining where to begin, which expert to believe, and which trend to follow, quickly becomes daunting, which might prompt you back to the sidelines where it's safe.

But know that your greater risk lies in standing still. To prompt you into action—or more directed action if you're already actively marketing within the digital space—and to give you a starting place to learn some core strategies about social media and decide the value for yourself, we begin with a bit of a different context than the one being offered by many social media developers, commentators, and salespeople today. Specifically, objective, strategy and tactics are still what count most when it comes to smart marketing, public relations and corporate communications.

So when you hear senior leadership clamoring for social media tools simply because "everybody else is doing it," stop to consider if these tools really can add value to your organization and also the level of corporate commitment behind them.

If the value is real—and there is plenty out there—and the resources are solid, then by all means, full speed ahead! But if you find yourself back at "everyone else is doing it" as your best or only reason for trying out these tools, our recommendation is that you return to the strategy room until a more viable rationale has surfaced.

We cannot overemphasize that the time you spend planning— methodically, strategically, and quantitatively—will be worth the month or two spent fretting about not having an active Facebook page, or worse yet, activating a Facebook page and not knowing what to do with it. Your first order of business must be getting to know the social media spaces in which your consumers are spending time, and to get to know social media as both consumer and creator.

We will cover a great deal of ground pertaining to social media applications, but know that each area that we discuss is worthy of (and is) a book unto itself. We'll leave the full-blown explorations of how to set up an account on Twitter to the site, itself, partly because new iterations of and updates to applications emerge with such frequency, that walking you through the Facebook sign-on page, or how to create a site using Ning could be out of date before you even make it to the end of the chapter.

Instead, we'll focus on our area of expertise, which is shaping marketing and communications strategies that will optimize your business objectives quickly and painlessly.

If you are still lukewarm on the idea of social media and the seemingly endless effort involved, let us introduce you to Dave Carroll. If you've ventured onto YouTube any time in recent months—or have friends keeping you in the loop on this type of content—you may have already met Dave, a man who best exemplifies what all the fuss is about in the social media space.

Dave started out as an everyday passenger who, when on a routine flight from Nova Scotia to Nebraska, had the unfortunate experience of having his $3,500 Taylor guitar damaged by United Airlines' baggage handlers. After more than a year of frustrated attempts to have the airline make amends, Carroll, a Canadian country music singer took matters into his own hands by making a four-minute-and-thirty-seven-second video depicting his trials and tribulations with the airline.

The video, with its catchy tune, engaging jokes and compelling lyrics, was posted to YouTube on July 6, 2009. Less than 24 hours later, it had racked up 24,000 views. And then it went truly viral. Too late to avoid public outcry at its initial lack of response, but before the video even got close to its nearly 5 million views (and counting!), United Airlines started to care. And this is why your company needs to care.

And yet, it needs to care in a manner that is strategic and well planned. Almost every corporation is running at social media at top speed without stopping to ask why, and the result can sometimes be surprising. Like a sudden rainstorm on the freeway, where drivers begin swerving, speeding up, and crashing for no good reason other than knee-jerk driver error, social media has a way of inadvertently causing corporations to do stupid things.

Social media is not a secret-weapon strategy, and it's not a magic bullet. It's merely a set of tactics—tactics that have the added benefit of forcing marketers to shed many of the practices that weren't working in the first place.

2

Social Media Boot Camp

WHEN WE SPEAK IN FRONT of audiences large and small and ask how many people are currently using social media, nearly every hand flies into the air. When we ask how many can define social media, the hands come down in rapid succession. This is often followed by chuckles and sheepish grins in that they realize what many companies are finding out the hard way: Being a user of social media is different from understanding what it is and how it functions as a marketing, public relations and communications tool.

In *Join the Conversation* (2007), Joseph Jaffe writes that "social media is a commitment, not a campaign."[1] We extrapolate one step further to say that social media is a *long-term* commitment, requiring top-down support, resources (financial and human) and a willingness to see the efforts through. Despite its proclaimed characteristics of being instantaneous and of cutting through

---

[1] Joseph Jaffe. *Join the Conversation: How to Engage Marketing-Weary Consumers with the Power of Community, Dialogue, and Partnership*, (Hoboken, NJ, John Wiley & Sons Inc., January 2008).

the intermediaries to drive straight to the hearts and minds of consumers, this is more the ideal, and at times an oversimplification of how social media can work on behalf of your brand.

In fact, your efforts in the social media space could easily take just as long as any other tactic, depending upon your company, your audience and your target market's palatability for this form of communication.

In essence, social media are online platforms, applications or distribution channels designed to engage target groups and to facilitate interaction, sharing and collaboration—all of which are centered on content. Unlike other forms of media, such as traditional television or static pre-Web 2.0 websites, social media's claim to fame is that it is customizable, portable, time-shifted and endlessly shareable, offering a constant connection to concentric circles of online communities.

The psychological appeal to users is that they (we) like to be seen as the ones in the know, with cutting-edge content that the communities who matter may not yet have discovered. You likely have one of these individuals in your office—you may be this individual—who routinely sends around links to articles perceived to have value to coworkers. When the articles prove themselves to be valuable time and again, the sender establishes him or herself as a credible source and a value-added member of the group.

As information consumers, we revel in being the ones who found the information first, so we rush to share it with our colleagues, superiors, friends and families. In this regard, the marketing work for any brand has never been easier now that forces on the ground are more than willing to spread the word about an industry trend, a tremendous product, a great deal, or a little-known company that offers outstanding service.

The downside, of course, is that these same users will not be shy about providing their less-than-positive word-of-mouth remarks, sharing thoughts and opinions on the worst products out there, the shoddiest customer-service practices and the most dreadful results with said-to-be-quality offerings. And in the social media space, both the positives and the negatives stick.

Despite this risk, brand managers are willing to take their chances—some of their own volition, others, realizing that either way, their brands may be at risk.

The job of any organization that enters the social media space is to create buzz by making the message, value proposition, or product offering compelling and easy to share. But social media, like other channels, is just one of many tactics that should comprise an overall strategy.

The benefits of social media are that it is a relatively inexpensive way to reach the public and offers the ability to build brand awareness, spread messages rapidly, generate "brand ambassadors," drive leads and revenue, and leverage existing social networks of engaged consumers. Some of the magic lies in its ability to create ongoing, real-time feedback loops that can be used to gauge input on core messaging, brand enhancements, new products, consumer ideas and opinions.

To get it right, social media must be centered on authentic messaging that is communicated in the language of the audience. Does this mean you must forego all signs of your brand in favor of the middle-aged men who love Harleys that you are trying to engage? No. But it does mean peeling back the layers of institution-speak that may have mired your brand for decades, and instead uncovering a clear, consistent, believable and sustainable corporate voice. Establishing this credibility will enable you to create a real, emotional connection with your target groups because in part, it will enable you to personalize the brand experience like never before.

To the old adage that it's not what you say but how you say it, we would add, and "when you say it" that counts. Sending the right message to the right person at the right time is the goal.

So, for example, when Krispy Kreme in Albuquerque, NM (@KrispyKremeABQ) sends a tweet for a half-price special on a dozen donuts—and we receive this on our commute to work, which causes us to realize that we do have a meeting and a quick sugar-fix would be appreciated by our hardworking staff—we see a model of the type of connection that will enable your brand to drive further into the psyche of consumers than ever before.

How will you know your tweet about a promotion, upcoming event, or contest is being well-received? Like everything else, being effective in this space is about effectively listening, tracking and then modifying your message as needed.

Social media is part public relations, part direct response, part brand marketing, part customer intelligence and part sales support with no single group being accountable. Very few organizations have an integrated approach and yet, social media provides the perfect storm to rally your troops and catapult results.

THE NEW "A" TEAM: MARKETING, COMMUNICATIONS AND PUBLIC RELATIONS

If you work at a company in which marketing, communications and public relations have long lived in harmony, lucky you. If you work in an environment in which marketing does its thing, while corporate communications is the group responsible for cranking out the quarterly newsletter, while public relations is focused more narrowly on fielding calls from the media and pushing major company news, heads up: Now's the time to get to know your counterparts.

If your PR team is tweeting about an upcoming event, as a marketer you want a piece of that. If your corporate communications group is shaping a new eblast campaign, your Facebook page should be set up as a direct link and included as a standard component on all of your communications. Tearing down walls and creating synergies amongst these groups has been a longstanding battle cry, so this isn't new. But what is new is that now—weekly poker night with the PR team or not—your pools and streams have begun to spill into one another. This can be a big win for any company.

If not attended to, however, you can be faced with a sea change that leaves you soaking wet and missing the mark. For example, take one of the most famous cases of viral video marketing: Mentos-Coke. As the story has been endlessly recounted, in 2006, a professional juggler and an attorney made a video of their Mentos-Coke experiment, in which the dropping of the confections into the soda causes a fun-to-watch geyser effect. The pair then uploaded the video to YouTube. A viral hit, the video was subsequently downloaded more than 20 million times, with 10,000 copycat videos.

But that's not the interesting part of the story.

The real takeaway is the corporate response. On the Mentos side, VP of marketing, Pete Healy offered, "We are tickled pink by it."

On Coca Cola's end, the response from spokeswoman Susan McDermott was starkly different, when she offered, "We would hope people want to drink Diet Coke more than try experiments with it ... the craziness with Mentos ... doesn't fit with the brand personality of Diet Coke."

After a 5-10% uptick in sales, Coke's interactive marketers changed the company's tune and in 2007, supplied unlimited product to the pair, and relaunched Coke's website with the Mentos-Coke geysers.

But as with all things Web 2.0, the damage was done in that the story of Coke's initial reaction lives on. In fact, Google "Mentos-Coke" today and you'll find articles still bemoaning Coke's out-of-it response. The takeaway: Online content is pervasive and resurfacing, so a thoughtful response that a company is willing to live with for the long haul—in this case a combined marketing-public relations-corporate communications response—must become more the rule than the exception.

Your consumers aren't stopping to ask where the lines of your departments are drawn as they rate your product, blog on your service or tweet about your tremendous discounts on tableware. The rules of engagement have changed from the outside in, and the smart corporations are using this merged pool to their advantage.

To take the rules of where you are and what you do a bit further, in the social media realm, your communicators and consumers must include internals (employees, stakeholders, shareholders) and externals (consumers, media, general public), at times serving in reverse roles. For example, on Best Buy's Blue Shirt Nation blog, employees engage with one another and consumers in brand new engagements; employees on their personal blogs associating themselves with their company, but noting their expression as a personal opinion—but nevertheless including such content as railing against planned new products that they see as inherently "flawed").

The corporate mix needs to center on creating an umbrella housing intersections of marketing and communications activities across an organization. Depending upon how your organization is structured, this can include one or all of the following:

- Public Relations
- Media Relations
- Investor Relations
- Marketing and Advertising
- Brand Management
- Corporate Identity
- Corporate Reputation Management
- Crisis Communication
- Employee Communication

Social media presents these "touchpoint" professionals with unique opportunities to employ synergistic tactics for engagement across publics. Of course, on the opposite end of the spectrum, social media presents unique challenges to ensuring clear objectives for each public and best practices for reaching these groups.

Within this context, social media must be predicated on a long-term, integrated communications strategy, and benefits and risks must be assessed prior to any social media engagement. We cannot overstate that all social media activities must be based on clear and well-defined business objectives.

To begin, you'll need to be realistic about costs (e.g., tracking, outside consultants, etc.). Moreover, you'll need to be realistic about energy, existing skill sets and experience of the staff who will be executing your social media plan. The myth of instant viral success really is just that. The notion that you'll launch a clever video and receive six million hits in two weeks is, in most cases, unreasonable. As the saying goes, it may take years to become an overnight success—even in the rapid-fire, viral world of social media.

This is where social media optimization comes into play. We'll leave social media optimization and search engine optimization intricacies to the experts in those areas, but we will set forth this advice: Social media optimization (SMO) works for organizations like search engine optimization (SEO) works for the Internet—so you'll want to make this a part of your plan.

While SEO is a process of employing keywords and associated searches to grow the volume and the quality of traffic to a website from organic or paid search results (the higher your company's site ranks in a search engine, the more searchers will visit your site), SMO is based on mathematically derived models of influence designed to determine the strength of the opinion leaders within a social network. In other words, SMO can offer ways of building efficiencies into the methods used for disseminating messages to consumers.

SEO and SMO aside, social media has the ability to generate brand awareness, product awareness and most importantly, revenue. Based on a study conducted in July 2009 by Charlene Li of the Altimer Group, which scored the engagement level of each of the top 100 brands across more than 10 social media channels (e.g., blogs, Facebook, Twitter, wikis and discussion forums), the top 10 brands most engaged in social media are: 1. Starbucks; 2. Dell; 3. eBay; 4. Google; 5. Microsoft; 6. Thomson Reuters;

7. Nike; 8. Amazon; 9. SAP; and 10. Yahoo!/Intel (These brands tied for tenth place).[2]

While the list may have changed since the study was conducted, it does provide a solid picture of the diversity of corporate interests engaged in the social media space. Each employs social media tactics in slightly different ways and in different combinations, but all are focused on increasing engagement and moving the dial on their bottom line.

As for which department within a given company "owns" social media, the answer here, too, ranges dramatically based on the organization. Generally speaking, within corporate and non-profit organizations alike, social media ownership has fallen to the following groups in priority order:

1.   Customer service
2.   Marketing
3.   Public relations

Other groups to become involved include Legal, Investor Relations, Human Resources and the employees, themselves. And as social media continues to evolve, departmental ownership will continue to shift. In addition to ascertaining who in your company will be leading the social media charge, you'll first want to take into account some core considerations.

Before entering a social network, you'll want to gain some insights into the types of social networks in which your customers are already engaged. Are most of your customers using Facebook?

---

[2] B. Elowitz and C. Li, "The world's most valuable brands. Who's most engaged?" (July 2009). Full Report found at http://www.engagementdb.com/downloads/ENGAGEMENTdb_Report_2009.pdf

Do only a handful know Twitter beyond the reference in a joke they may catch on the late show?

Ask this question up front, and avoid the disappointment of tweeting in the wind or finding yourself fan-less. If your target group is not currently engaged within a social network, you'll need to determine if and how you might migrate your existing base onto these networks to better reach them. (Read: If you build it, they will *not* come, unless you give them plenty of promotion and a value-added reason).

Should you be fortunate enough to have located the groups you'd like your brand to connect with, you'll then need to determine in which networks, at what point, and how you might enter their conversations. Just because you are a mega-brand (e.g., Apple or Disney), doesn't mean a community of engaged users necessarily wants you in its space.

You'll need to listen first, by monitoring the types of activity and conversations that are taking place, ask if outreach would be okay, and then tread lightly at first, armed with a sense of the types of messages the existing group will—or will not—accept. Before you ask permission to enter an existing group's space, be prepared with a plan for ongoing engagement. The worst strategy you could employ is to storm a user-generated network, only to fall silent for lack of a strategic plan for continued conversation.

3

Psychology of Social Media Survival

F OR THOSE WHO CAN EMBRACE the inevitability of technological changes, social media represents one of the greatest opportunities of this young century.

As Paul Gillin noted in *The New Influencers* (2009),[1] we've gone from one-way directional messages to conversations. From the origins of the Web 1.0 platform (derived Star Wars prequel style— that is, only in response to Web 2.0), we have become an audience craving interactivity and engagement.

Web 1.0 was comprised of corporate brochureware sites and based on one-to-many messaging. You'll still find such sites around, though chances are you won't encounter any traffic jams in getting there.

For those of you who are too far gone in the Web 2.0 platform to remember—or simply too new to the scene—Web 1.0 sites contain limited interactivity inviting users, for example, to fill out

---

[1] Paul Gillin. *The New Influencers*, (Sanger, CA: Quill Driver Books/Word Dancer Press, Inc., June 2007).

a very basic form. And you'll find limited sharing on these sites as well, such as "E-mail this to a friend." Remember the days of the sole envelope icon on a select few sites containing articles?

The customization was limited as well, where perhaps you might see, "Welcome, Joan Smith" at the top of the page. Beyond that, the customer received standard-issue fare.

In Web 2.0, a term generally attributed to Tim O'Reilly of the O'Reilly Media Group, the advent of do-it-yourself publishing, such as blogging and podcasting, coupled with social networking or socialcasting sites such as MySpace and Facebook created a new breed of content known as User-Generated Content (UGC) or Consumer-Generated Content (CGC).

This launched a series of terms you may be hearing ad nauseam—social media, interactivity, shareability. Depending on how vested or disinterested your organization is, you may be more or less familiar with the catch phrases.

The trouble for many corporations is that they feel if they don't know by now, it's too late to admit their ignorance. For organizations with a corporate image that says "cutting edge" or "first to market," a lapse in social media aptitude can feel like a devastating blow to the brand.

Many companies have begun to equate social media aptness with the core of the brand, itself. Knowing that the social media train has long since left the station, the idea of leaving the super-cool brand behind at a deserted terminal has caused an avalanche of poorly planned and even more poorly executed social media strategies.

Know going in that (a) there are more people with you at the station than you may think; and (b) there is always a jumping-in point to any new media, at any point along the way in its evolution.

If you don't believe us, consider the realm of the World Wide Web. Remember when your company did not have a website? Perhaps you can recall the days in which your customer feedback surveys were sent via fax instead of e-mail. If you've been through the web evolution and made it through, you'll get through the Web 2.0 evolution having already experienced one dramatic and irreversible shift.

Websites and applications with community functionality and customizable media consumption (e.g., personalized music playlists, iGoogle, Netvibes, etc.) demand that communications professionals rethink existing paradigms.

Whereas the job of the marketing and communications professional once centered on creating messages, delivering push mechanisms to the marketplace and constructing campaigns, the Web 2.0 paradigm insists on a philosophy reengineered to reflect such tasks as developing consumer connections, developing pull interactions and replacing the well-orchestrated campaign with facilitating conversations. This leaves many feeling somewhat out of their comfort zones.

Why? Because as communications professionals, we've been taught that controlling the message is our top order of business. That policing the brand and sending forth precise messages at precise times for precise target groups was the stuff that would one day get us promoted in the industry.

In the wake of the Web 2.0 paradigm shift, these are the very elements that are causing angst amongst professionals. In essence, the social media framework insists upon relinquishing—or at the very least, sharing—control of the message with the ranks of consumers. No talking points. No planned press conferences. The content is now being generated real time, any time, in the space in which consumers congregate. So if you think you're not joining in for fear of putting your brand at risk, think again: It's at risk either way.

So, we know why *WE* are engaging in social media—to reach audiences faster, to listen and engage, to build our brands, and to increase our profits. But why are *THEY* engaging?

The psychological drivers behind social media are not necessarily complex. In fact, in some respects, they are downright rudimentary, but they bear repeating to exemplify the fact that nothing much has changed in the new media space. To begin with, people want a sense of belonging. Maslow's hierarchy of needs is never far away, nor is the desire to satisfy the basic need of being a part of something.

Next, is the need for self-expression. Quite simply, people want a voice, and they want that voice to be heard. This is a feature that people really didn't have access to in the world of Web 1.0. By way of analogy, step into any break room on a Monday morning, or catch a group in an elevator, and you'll hear the same thing: People telling their stories. From weekend soccer, to a gig in a Bluegrass band, to irritating mother-in-laws to family pets, people want to tell their stories and they want to hear what others have to say. Transferring this to your corporate brand, people likewise enjoy serving as advocates for products, brands and services about which they feel passionately—the downside being that passion swings both ways.

Hence, in the social media space, individuals across a diverse demographic are creating profiles expressing who they are. This expression can be both liberating and frightening at the same time. Liberating for organizations because with the creation of a blog or a Facebook page, they are "out there" and sharing a part of themselves with a broader community. Frightening, because with the creation of a blog or a Facebook page, organizations are "out there" and sharing a part of themselves with a broader community. Criticism. Praise. Negative comments. Creepy followers. Exciting new pipeline of prospects. Panned reviews. This is risk and reward, and it's a package deal. To date, corporations who are active in social media fall into one of two categories: Either they are willing to embrace the risks—or they simply haven't thought about the risks.

Important to keep in mind is that the price of unlimited bandwidth to tell your story is unlimited public consumption, which by nature violates rights to privacy. Thus, things meant to be private should never be placed in this public space.

And yet, as marketers, we must give users/consumers ample opportunity and ability to create as much content—particularly surrounding our brand—as they desire.

Humans have an innate need to be seen as important. We all enjoy this because it makes us feel satisfied, valued and worthy of being a part of the communities in which we strive to be included. The social media space gives us some wonderful tools with which to facilitate for people the ability to influence others. If you've ever recommended a product, chatted in a discussion group, rated a product, or taken a poll, you'll know what we mean.

The simple act of voting on which celebrity has the worst track record for cheating on a spouse, or being able to comment on that pair of four-inch stiletto heels that NO WOMAN SHOULD WEAR EVER AGAIN—EVER—gives people a definite sense of power. Social media gives a voice to a dramatically broad range of people: those who may be too shy to complain to a restaurant manager about the bad service they received can go home and blog about it. The catchword of engagement is "I have a say."

STORYTELLING 3.0

The discipline of communication is fascinating because it takes the best of psychology and sociology and a range of cross-disciplinary elements and thus, is able to explain phenomena of human behavior in as neat a package as human behavior might be expected to fit. Walter Fisher first set forth his theory of narration as a human communication paradigm in 1984. Fisher's Narrative Paradigm is centered on the notion that humans are storytellers, and that values, emotions and aesthetic considerations ground our beliefs in behaviors.

Hence, according to the theory, people are persuaded more by intriguing stories than by logical arguments alone. Fisher believed that all meaningful communication is storytelling in one form or another and that life, itself, is a series of narratives, with all the elements of a story: from antagonists and protagonists, to high drama, suspense, humor and action, to a beginning, a middle and an end. Offering a great beginning to a story is where social media can become a most powerful muse on behalf of the brand it serves.

Technology has enabled us to be collaborative storytellers in a new and exciting way. From Storytelling 1.0 and the oral tradition, to Storytelling 2.0 beginning with Guttenberg's printing press and evolving into mass-mediated distribution of ideas through radio, television and Web 1.0, we've arrived at Storytelling 3.0 in which interactivity and shareability are the commodities of the story.

User comments, recommendations of products, the sharing of playlists and aggregated sets of links, posts and favorites—these are the stories of today's brands. You job as a communicator is to offer starting points designed to encourage dialogue, shape communities and foster brand loyalty. So while the act of storytelling has changed to include users and consumers, corporate communications still maintains a vital role as the story starter for many-to-many communications.

Now anyone can be a publisher (a storyteller), so competition for consumers is fierce: from blogging to podcasting, to video and print-on-demand. We must keep in mind that the ratio of publishers to readers has increased dramatically with Do-It-Yourself (DIY) publishing technologies.

Bloggers, visitors to social media sites, anyone in the digital conversation can keep a story going in an iterative, viral process. This means, of course, the good stories and the bad.

Commentary, including reviews and ratings, can affect the brand story (product) or the publisher story (the outlet that disseminates the story) long after the story prompt, itself, has come and gone. Coca-Cola's "Coke Zero" blog showcases this best. In November 2005, Coke attempted to reach a targeted demographic, which prompted the creation of a blog. Problematically, the blog was alleged to have been created by a regular Coke Zero fan. In less time than it takes to drink a can of the stuff, the Coke Zero fan blog was outed as nothing more than a shameless and deceptive corporate ploy.

The aftermath of this story starter was far worse than the blunder itself, prompting the creation of a site titled, "The Zero Movement Sucks." To this day, do a search for "Coke Zero" and you'll quickly uncover the backlash blogs. Like the endless recounting from family members of when, at two-and-a-half you ran boldly through the neighborhood wearing nothing but a cape and shouting, "Superman is here!" these stories refuse to stay buried, much to companies' chagrin. Above all else, Web 2.0 is definitely sticky.

The business of storytelling centers on defining the story as information—any piece of information. Website publishers want to be seen as the go-to place to read a certain type of "story," which can be content that they create themselves or content that they aggregate. Not only are the brochureware sites no longer effective, but people have come to expect free information that they can comment on, add to and share—and THEN they will buy your product or return to your site if the experience was good.

Content creators want as many visitors as possible to travel to their sites in order to keep up with the evolving story or add their commentary to evolve the story. The more the story is viewed and commented on, the more opportunities to monetize with ads or sell the visitor a product or service.

But lest you let the waves of the blogosphere or the user-generated-content movement lull you into thinking that main-stream news has gone away, it's important to note that news outlets continue to play the main role of story starter by publishing a text article, a photo or a video.

Amidst the ongoing debate as to whether bloggers are journal-ists, one answer is clear at the moment: Bloggers and journalists can sometimes achieve the same results, and bloggers and journal-ists can derive a great deal of value from one another—but the two groups remain distinct. As a case in point, professional journalists still make up nearly the entirety of the Presidential press pool (several noted bloggers were admitted into the pool during the

Obama administration). Journalists continue to function as the gatekeepers to our world, and thus, the gatekeepers to content for the blogosphere, a fact that should not be overlooked.

Growing a story can take the form of a citizen journalist or blogger who adds to a story with observations. It can take the form of any site visitor who comments on the story. Brand advertisers are part of this mix: They pitch their stories in ways designed to kindle ongoing dialogue. These "stories" can include Facebook fan pages, videos, white papers, ads and widgets. Each tells a story and ideally creates, through often disparate elements, a holistic picture of your brand.

Important to remember is integration. Creating a Facebook account, but failing to promote this aggressively across all media will not get you far. For each social media tool, you must devise a marketing strategy to drive users toward that space. This is where content can help. The key is to create a strong piece of content, then publish it multiple times in flexible formats.

If you can pool your content into an aggregated format (e.g., an archive of best practices for tropical fish owners, or seasonal tips on tending a rose garden), you will have created a rich repository and thus a great reason for people to flock to your main objective, which is likely centered on selling tropical fish supplies or rosebushes.

Another ready patch of quicksand is the desire of corporations to create their own unique social networking space. Everyone from cereal makers to feminine hygiene products has jumped on this bandwagon, but the results can be sketchy. Keep in mind that most consumers will have one—and just one—primary social networking space that they devote their energies to on a regular basis. It's simply not feasible for most people to devote time to the upkeep of multiple sites.

Hence, if you are considering creating a space outside of existing networks, know where your audience engages first and you'll spend less time shaking your head about why your amazing site on Florida grapefruits has gone unnoticed. If your Florida grapefruit site on Facebook has yielded a plethora of requests for a separate space, then consider your next move—or better yet, simply let your audiences do their thing and create their own separate site devoted to promoting the glories of the grapefruit.

In sum, be sure of the level of commitment before you begin. If you think you are going to launch big and find support later, think again. Adding social media tools to your arsenal involves real time and real money. Once you create a space, it's yours for the long haul.

Remember, too, that the only thing worse than not being in the social media space, is stagnating in the social media space. If you launch a campaign in MySpace in a set-it-and-forget-it fashion, you have just created a recurring negative for your brand by associating your corporate name with an abandoned site. Avoid this at all costs.

The notion that consumer influence shapes brands, but brands no longer shape consumers is only partially true. To relinquish full control of your brand to your consumers would be folly, but to shape strategy and content knowing there will be additional hands in the dough before the brand is fully baked is a sound approach.

Walmart

One telling case of consumer-corporate shaping of a brand is Walmart. In the social media space, Walmart has taken a number of hits over the years. In 2006, in perhaps its most notorious adventure in social media, consumers began taking note of a blog titled, "Wal-Marting Across America"—the work of a couple of friends who took their RV across country and happened to blog about their stops at Walmart stores along the way. Shortly thereafter, and as the blogosphere goes, readers started asking questions, which turned up the fact that the regular Joe and Jane were actually two paid freelance writers. And their fabulous shots of the stores? Captured by a paid freelance photographer.

One might be inclined to let Walmart slide a bit on this one— the space was new and perhaps the message that authenticity really does matter was not quite taken to heart. After all, we have long been riding on the institutionally controlled message, so we'll give them a pass on the premise that old habits can be hard to break.

Undaunted, they got back up and in that same year, Walmart created a social networking site called The Hub. The Walmart version of MySpace, this site was designed as a meeting place for tweens who could come together in an online space to talk about fashion, fads and all things tween. The problem here was that those tweens who might have gone to MySpace…simply went to MySpace (For more on The Hub, see Chapter 25).

Like a Phoenix, Walmart rose in 2007, having learned from its experiences, to create a Facebook site designed for college-aged students to convene and to take part in a "style test" whereby based on their responses they would be shown their ideal dorm style. But the strategy of engagement wasn't fully sketched out, and in the end, interest in the site fizzled faster than a weekly print circular, and this attempt also failed—which brought the company to 2009 and its "elevenmoms" blog.

Like the Mentos-Coke account, in which the more telling positioning stems from the mouths of the corporate executives, here is what Walmart posted by way of friendly blogosphere context, prefacing its launch of a new blog designed for moms:[2]

> We began slowly, making contacts in Twitter, leveraging Facebook profiles, viewing related YouTube videos, and trying to understand how we could participate. And not just by adding more messaging. We made friends. We heard from our critics. And we began to interact as both Walmart associates and as people.
>
> We began to reach out to some of the bloggers we had been following to find out if they would be interested in building a connected money saving community.
>
> In all we invited eleven Mom Bloggers to participate and began to refer to the group as "elevenmoms." Several Moms strongly suggested that we add another Mom Blogger that they regarded highly so we did. Hence, we have 12 "elevenmoms," a great value as well!
>
> We are honored to be able to work with this great group of Moms.

Those who are particularly tuned in to rhetorical devices might offer that the above belies an ongoing reluctance to relinquish

---

[2] ElevenMoms Blog, http://instoresnow.walmart.com/Community.aspx, www.elevenmoms.com

brand-speak in favor of real engagement, but the jury is still out on the success of their latest endeavor.

In the meantime, consumers have been busy, themselves, when it comes to representing Walmart. A rogue, yet popular website (Peopleofwalmart.com) has emerged, dedicated to the pursuit of capturing in photos what they deem to be the essence of Walmart-shopper style.

Hence, we have a site with some of the most outlandish and unfortunately real images of store shoppers wearing everything from Army fatigues and bare midriffs to bedroom slippers. Not exactly what Walmart was driving for, and yet, to date this consumer-generated site is perhaps the most authentic Walmart yet.

The takeaway is that consumers aren't asking first; they're simply taking the lead. "Blog first, ask questions later" is the new consumer mantra.

Technology is enabling users to consume their media whenever (time-shifting) and wherever (multi-platform) they'd like. The principle behind User-Generated Content (UGC) is that users now expect to both consume and create.

Best Buy

Best Buy's Blue Shirt Nation (BSN) blog provides an example of "resetting the top" so that the story spins in favor of your brand. Best Buy's Chief Marketing Officer, Barry Judge, began a post with these words:

We recently posted a job that got a lot of buzz because of its qualifications. The Senior Manager, Emerging Media Marketing role had among the qualifications, one year of active blogging experience, and preferred qualifications of a graduate degree, and 250+ followers on Twitter.[3]

His original job posting had received negative commentary from the job applicants, themselves. But Judge turned this potential negative into an engagement opportunity in which he invited readers to offer their ideas for this job description. He then invited the group to select the description they thought was best, thus avoiding the negative PR of what the public perceived to be unreasonable job qualifications—and replacing this with community empowerment.

Users can no doubt influence the development of brands through personal opinions, as consumers—and even job candidates—are flexing their muscle in never-before-seen ways. It's not so much that marketers are losing control, but the days of policing the brand as untouchable are definitely gone. Marketers must come to terms with the "please touch" mentality when it comes to their brands, because, counterintuitive though it may seem, it may be just what the brand ordered.

---

[3] Barry Judge, "Help us write the job description" (Updates from the CMO of Best Buy, July 2009).
http://barryjudge.com/help-us-write-the-job-description-sr-manager-emerging-media-marketing

4

The Strategy of Engagement:
Your Social Media Policy

E HAVE HEARD organizations say that they are not yet "ready" for a social media policy, but that perhaps they will revisit the idea in a year or so. Considering that social media years are like dog years, 12 months from now may be too late.

In fact, your company's social media policy must be created from the outset not only to offer some guidelines for users, but also as a means of formalizing the corporate commitment—at least an initial one—to social media. Further, those who experiment first and create the ground rules later are usually the ones who spend more time mopping up social media messes than actually employing these tactics as a means of enhancing consumer touch-points.

On the employees' side, doing the right thing when it comes to using social networking really isn't hard. Yet it has cost people their jobs, and their hard-earned reputations, and sometimes any prospects of a future job. Social media can be ruthless that way.

We're asked all the time about balance in the workplace. Employees want to know how to balance their corporate image and their personal brand—or more often—just their personal form of expression. This is part and parcel of your company's social media policy.

There are two sides to consider when it comes to establishing a social media policy: The risks to your brand, and the risks to your employees. A sound social media policy will minimize both types of risk.

On the employee side, using social media effectively without compromising one's job is mostly about understanding the tools being used, and the impact they have.

New employees—or longtime employees active in the social media space—should get into the habit of asking about their company's social media policy at the outset. Companies who do have policies on employee use of social media run the gamut from being broad-based to being so narrow that the policy becomes more of a means of stymieing any potential community building that might be taking place.

Some social media policies are a bit more restrictive than others. Take *The Washington Post*:

> *All Washington Post journalists relinquish some of the personal privileges of private citizens. Post journalists must recognize that any content associated with them in an online social network is, for practical purposes, the equivalent of what appears beneath their bylines in the newspaper or on our website.*

What you do on social networks should be presumed to be publicly available to anyone, even if you have created a private account. It is possible to use privacy controls online to limit access to sensitive information. But such controls are only a deterrent, not an absolute insulator. Reality is simple: If you don't want something to be found online, don't put it there.[1]

Or ESPN:

• *Personal websites and blogs that contain sports content are not permitted*

• *Prior to engaging in any form of social networking dealing with sports, you must receive permission from the supervisor as appointed by your department head*

• *ESPN.COM may choose to post sports related social media content*

• *If ESPN.com opts not to post sports related social media content created by ESPN talent, you are not permitted to report, speculate, discuss or give any opinions on sports related topics or personalities on your personal platforms*

• *The first and only priority is to serve ESPN sanctioned efforts, including sports news, information and content*

---

[1] *The Washington Post*'s Social Media Guidelines can be found at:
http://paidcontent.org/article/419-wapos-social-media-guidelines-paint-staff-into-virtual-corner/

• *Assume at all times you are representing ESPN*

• *If you wouldn't say it on the air or write it in your column, don't tweet it*

• *Exercise discretion, thoughtfulness and respect for your colleagues, business associates and our fans*

• *Avoid discussing internal policies or detailing how a story or feature was reported, written, edited or produced and discussing stories or features in progress, those that haven't been posted or produced, interviews you've conducted, or any future coverage plans.*

• *Steer clear of engaging in dialogue that defends your work against those who challenge it and do not engage in media criticism or disparage colleagues or competitors*

• *Be mindful that all posted content is subject to review in accordance with ESPN's employee policies and editorial guidelines*

• *Confidential or proprietary company information or similar information of third parties who have shared such information with ESPN, should not be shared*

Any violation of these guidelines could result in a range of consequences, including but not limited to suspension or dismissal.[2]

Keep in mind that the ideal policy should not read like a social media buzz kill, it is a primer on best practices. Remember, we're trying to gain advocates within the company as much as we are trying to avoid undue risk.

One of the problems that employees face is failing to treat the community in which they work with dignity and respect. If you think posting a daily update on the state of your lousy job and your horrible boss are safe on your Facebook fan page, think again. Remember that shareability means just that. Even a fairly benign comment about "lazy coworkers" can cause a furor—and can position an employee as anything but a team player.

Transparency is what makes the social media world go around. This means that if you permit personal blogs on topics related to your company or industry, and you have an employee who blogs about the dismal state of Smith Supermarkets' produce, she will need to mention that she works for Jones' Supermarkets across town. At the very least, you will want to note that employees who blog on related topics outside of their professional positions will, at the very least, need to include a note that "the information on this blog is based on my own personal opinion, and does not represent the opinion of my employer, Jones' Supermarkets."

Further, employees should post and blog responsibly, understanding that public space is just that—public. Anyone who tells you that what you do in social media on your time is your own

---

[2] ESPN's Social Media Policy can be found at:
http://profootballtalk.nbcsports.com/2009/08/04/espns-guidelines-for-social-networking/

business just doesn't get it. An employee's right to express himself does not equate to a lack of consequences for saying something ill-fated or inappropriate that might become the brand's problem down the line.

Advice for employees who partake in all things social media: If you wouldn't want Mom to see it, don't put it out there. Photos of you dancing the tango on the top of a bar at your best friend's wedding may seem like a good idea when you post them—but trying frantically to delete them when your name pops up on your boss' Facebook page is not what you want to be doing.

On the brand side, the audience for your social media efforts is anybody. And everybody. And that's just it. At any point in time, the audience to your online presence might include current, past or potential clients, colleagues or employers. The problem is you'll never know for sure who's in the house. Consider all that you post and say in light of this—the last thing you want to do is insult, degrade or alienate. This goes for posting on the competition in particular. Social media has evolved an atmosphere in which competitor brands who find the most success are not smack-talking one another in competing social networks. Rather, they are holding conversations with each other and in the process, smartly tapping into competitor markets (e.g., Pepsi has been known to tweet to Coke, and vice versa).

Your policy should also set the boundary on humor. If your designated blogger has a borderline derogatory comment that he thinks followers would find amusing, your policy should be clear that he should not hit send, post or update.

Employees should refrain from comments that even hint at being insults. The goal of social media is not to create mini public relations crises, so be careful with content and its effects. Those using social media on behalf of the company and for personal purposes must understand that their employers can and will monitor their online activities. If you cringe at the thought of your manager seeing your Twitter account and those racy 140-character messages, stop before you tweet.

Your employees' online presences can brand them in ways they had never intentioned—the chauvinist, the drinker, the girl with all those boyfriends. The online presence an employee creates outside of work can become not only his or her biggest downfall— but an unwanted piece of publicity for your company as well.

Your social media policy should also speak to crediting sources appropriately. Sharing content does not negate the value of the copyright, and failing to cite the sources of your work is bad practice in any industry. Give credit where it is due, because the last thing you want is to have your company accused of passing off others' ideas as its own. Better to give a nod to a colleague or article—this approach will get you much farther in the long run.

Proprietary or confidential information should not be shared. This may seem like another no-brainer. And yet, it often becomes fodder for gray-area discussions. Showing our "authentic selves" in corporate social media does NOT mean revealing information before it is released—or sharing inside stories about the company not meant for public consumption. Transparency does not give employees free rein to share just anything. Employees who share confidential or proprietary information do so at the risk of losing their jobs and at times even winding up in the midst of a lawsuit.

Even an employee's inadvertent spill of corporate dish can place the company itself under public scrutiny as audiences cast judgment on the company's decision to place someone at the helm of communicating out who is unable to safeguard information.

The potential for missteps is real, so you will want to make sure this is clearly spelled out in your social media policy.

Further, your social media policy should contain a "no whiners or complainers" clause. Social media will only pay dividends for those who add value to followers, readers, fans and users—as opposed to those offering up gripes and complaints. This can be forgotten as social media point people let their guards down a bit in conversing with the public.

Lastly, your policy should include a "when" factor. If, for example, an employee tweets 14 times in a given day from her personal account—and she is not known as the tweeter for Big Brand X—the company may find itself faced with more unwanted public scrutiny on its employee productivity, human resources policy, etc. The general rule of thumb for social media policies is that employees not directly responsible for tweeting or blogging on behalf of their companies, should do so on their own time.

It is important to note that your social media policy is a working document that will evolve and grow as your company's efforts expand. And regardless of whether your company has established its own bank of data on risks and opportunities, sufficient data exists to suggest there is an established baseline of both. Basic best practices and risks are well-known—so better to stack the deck in your favor, and arm staff with this knowledge at the go point.

While social media calls for some non-traditional practices in terms of tone and theme, our experience has shown that even with more freedoms—or perhaps it is *because* of additional freedoms— staff have a greater comfort level entering the space on behalf of your organization when they know the ground rules.

Social media is more and more a part of the mainstream of corporate communications, marketing and public relations efforts.

If you're not yet convinced, you may have blinked. Even six months ago, the landscape of social media was less solidified, but with increased uses and applications, adoption rates continue to soar. But this doesn't mean that organizations are keeping pace in terms of figuring it all out.

In fact, the general strategy surrounding many social media implementations centers on the short-term sigh of relief that social media—any social media—is in place. Heads of marketing and communication have been charged with keeping up, becoming hip to new media, or simply staying in the race and are often relieved to find that someone in the office knows how to tweet. Hence, the social media office "expert" is born.

But that office expert who uses Facebook or MySpace, or knows his way around YouTube and the blogosphere might inadvertently channel his enthusiasm in ways that conflict with your company's brand or core mission. This is where a clear social media policy can be of great value.

If you uncover a stash of employees who are comfortable in the social media space, this means they are in that space for personal use. When asked to switch gears to become ambassadors of your brand, the transition may not be seamless. While tone and style are obvious question marks, aptitude for customer engagement is another factor worth considering before you send your troops out tweeting. It doesn't take social media to tell us that backroom analysts who are placed in front of clients might be a bit too forthcoming with the wrong message to consumers, or too technical, thus creating unintended issues that then need to be addressed.

And social media is a challenging beast to tame because just as it demands authenticity and sincerity, there's authenticity, and then there's authenticity. Thus, the urgent need for a social media policy that sets a solid framework of corporate expectations, along with the flexibility that employees need to go out and communicate without sounding like an institutional brochure. Employees need to know what's in scope and what's out of bounds. Because most will be communicating in a manner they haven't tried before— less formal, more conversational but still on brand (no pressure there)—you'll need to provide not only parameters, but sample messages that might serve as examples both of optimal communications and of communications best left on the cutting room floor.

Almost universally, social media policies must include a measure of awareness and education. Understanding that degrees of social media prowess vary dramatically—from those who are insulted that you ask if everyone is clear on the use of hashtags— to those who wake up in the middle of the night in a cold sweat, fearing that someone from senior leadership might stop them in the hallway to call them on the fact that they don't know MySpace from outer space.

Unlike other forms of corporate communications, in which employees are more than willing to "leave it to the experts," because social media began in the realm of the non-expert, this means that anyone who is not in the know feels at risk of being found out as foolish, out of touch, or as useful as an eight-track cassette tape. So your social media policy can also serve as a means of informing staff on social media in a more discreet way.

Ultimately, the goal is to empower employees without fostering an atmosphere of running with scissors. When it comes to social media, if you're going to do it right, you're going to need your forces on the ground to make it happen.

Areas to pay attention to start with tone and style (e.g., Will you allow a less formal tone?), levels of disclosure, types of content and topics that are in scope. Specifically, you'll want to create a policy that takes into account the creators, the consumers and the content itself.

Beginning with the creators, determine first who will be communicating based on your core brand objectives. What style or tone will your creators use? Will they tweet or blog using their individual names (@Sharon or @Michael)? Will you adopt an institutional presence (@YourBrandHere through which Sharon and Michael will share a schedule of tweeting?). This needs to be carefully considered at the onset to ensure employee comfort (some employees will prefer *not* to be personally associated with the corporate social media they will be asked to produce), as well as brand integrity (e.g., if Sharon becomes disgruntled and writes about this in her personal blog, is the blog immediately associated back to Sharon's communications on behalf of the brand?).

Whether the tone of your social media communicators is more institutional, fun, informative, friendly, academic or witty is based on the ultimate objective of the brand and the style that most aligns with and represents this brand. You may want a mix of voices, or several individuals, each with a distinctive tone and style. Be sure to consider the audience, and a tone and style that are appropriate for their expectations.

To best identify and enact your social media persona, you'll first want to understand who is out there in your social networking space (or that of your competitors) and what they are posting. If, for example, you are in the business of manufacturing high-end cookware, and you find that groups of bakers are generally commenting on the lack of customer service in the cookware world, or offer high praise for how one manufacturer maintains a 24/7 "pots 'n pans" hotline, you'll want to take these trends into account as you are establishing your guidelines based on the audience you are trying to attract.

As for content, itself, you must begin by identifying what's in and what's out.

Let's say, for example, you are a gourmet supermarket chain and your produce buyer blogs for the company on the latest in fruits and vegetables. If this employee maintains a personal blog and happens to mention the kumquats she discovered on a trip to the islands, she must be upfront and explain that she works for Gourmet-To-Go, but that her opinions on kumquats (or any other perishable she chooses to discuss) are her own, and not that of the company for whom she works and blogs.

Some examples include:

The opinions and positions expressed are my own and do not reflect those of Gourmet-To-Go.

Note: The content posted on this site is based on the author's personal opinion, and does not reflect the views of Gourmet-To-Go.

Or, to err on the extreme side of caution:

The opinions within this blog are based on my personal point of view. They are not the opinions of my employers, nor in any way does this blog, its entries, or any information on this site reflect the opinion of my employers or individuals associated with me.

When creating your organization's social media policy, keep in mind that this should be a fluid document that changes as technologies and applications change. Your guidelines should address content areas such as how to handle negative comments (e.g., leave them up, but address them within 24 hours; reserve the right to delete inappropriate, raunchy or downright offensive commentary ; etc.). They should also address whether personal comments and/ or quasi-personal remarks are in scope or not (e.g., discussions of your cat, Pepper, or the weather in South Bend, or the office holiday party to be held at the Four Seasons).

At the end of the day, your policy must speak to the core of any social media best practices: Adding value. Underlying any issues of tone, style or policy for acceptance or rejection of content, must be the value it adds to your audience. The question to ask is, "Does this content contribute to my brand?" If you can't find a "yes" then reconsider the content. Does it create community? Solve a problem? Foster a relationship with key opinion leaders? Answer a common question? Clarify a product feature? Then by all means, add this content to the conversation.

In effect, your social media policy should be more of a handbook for best practices than a carefully worded threat from the legal department.

That said, your policy needn't be long and filled with legalese. It does need to provide some clear guidance on such issues as what's in and what's out, when to disclose and when to withhold information, who to check with if you are unsure of acceptable content, and when it makes sense to check with legal first. Remembering that this is about customer engagement, the rules of that engagement should be set forth early, and should continue to evolve with the organization.

Interesting to note is that even our time-tested legalese has changed within the context of social media. For anyone in marketing who has ever had the pleasure of cleverly fitting in several paragraphs of fine print on something as seemingly benign as a kids' coloring contest, this example may make your heart sing. In conjunction with its contest rules pertaining to its 2009 #HoliDDay Twitter promotion, in which users were invited to tweet their thoughts on how Dunkin' Donuts helped "keep them running" during the holidays for a chance to win a $50 Dunkin' Donuts gift card, Dunkin' Donuts offered the obligatory legalese on its website—only with a delightful social media twist:

RULES FOR CONTESTS ON SOCIAL NETWORKS*

First thing you have to know is that our www.DunkinDonuts.com Terms of Use and Privacy Policy apply, except for any changes below. Know them. Live them. And check back here often as we may change these rules at any time.

The next thing is don't get too excited. What we are planning to give away (probably) won't make you rich, better looking, or famous.

If it isn't obvious, you don't have to buy anything to participate, play, or win. Any applicable taxes are on your nickel.

If we post a "Tweet" or message of the day, week, etc., or tell you we are going to pick our "fav" response to something, we get to pick the one we like. Period. Same applies when we say we are going to pick more than one.

If we offer something for the first number of "Tweets" or responses, we count based on when we received them. It's not our fault if computers or ISPs mess up, lose power, the dog eats your "Tweet", the dog eats our connection, the dog eats your computer, the dog eats you, etc., etc. If we want, we can allow more time, or cut short the time for responses.

Same deal if we ask for votes.

We also reserve the right to exclude a participant from contention if we deem your username, profile information, or your "Tweets" in general, to be offensive.

By playing, you give us permission to use your name and profile information to announce as a winner. If you want to know who won, visit the applicable site, but check quickly, as names won't be posted for long (about 2 days).

What you send us becomes our property.

Should you be lucky enough to win one of these contests, we will need to get some information from you in order to get you the prize that you won. If you don't give us enough information to contact you, we will move on.

Please don't play if you are 13-years-old or younger. Mom, Dad, or guardian will have to sign an affidavit for you if you are younger than 18.

Our employees, franchisees, vendors, and competitors can't win (our) prizes. If we ask, you have to confirm your eligibility.

Wait for it, wait for it, wait for it... here it comes: Void where pro-hibited!

That's that. Simple, right? [3]

We wish all legalese were as cheery and as cheeky as that.

Note: For links to sample social media policies across a range of companies and industries, see *Survival Kit: Links You Can Use* at the end of this book.

---

[3] https://www.dunkindonuts.com/contests/socialrules.aspx?cmpid=referral_000016

5

Assess the Corporate Commitment

I F YOUR PLAN IS TO EMBARK upon a full-court social media press within your organization, your first stop should be the C-Suite. Assess your company's commitment to social media, as honestly as possible, so that you'll know what you're getting into—and what type of support you can expect to receive. But don't let personal preferences serve as an indicator of corporate commitment.

Ed Whitacre, the newly appointed interim CEO of General Motors, for instance, does not have a computer in his office, and is no great fan of e-mail, but his commitment to social media—and frankly whatever type of media fosters dialogue and communication with employees and stakeholders—is strong, as noted by Mary Henige, Director of Social Media and Broadcast Communications at General Motors.

As a marketer, perhaps you've been faced with the peculiar situation of being approached by senior management with unreasonable demands for immediate leaps into social media. While the tactics themselves may turn out to be the most fabulous steps toward advancement your marketing team has ever created, the initial angst lies in the fact that often senior management isn't really sure what it is asking for—or why.

If you haven't yet had one of these conversations from someone in your organization, trust us, you will. If and when you do receive a request for something along the lines of "that Twitter thing" or "the Facebook," know that here is where your job as a professional becomes critical, in that you must first have the more sensitive conversation of ascertaining if the requestor knows what he or she is talking about.

This doesn't have to be a hard conversation, and in our experience, the baseline information you will need to determine your best recommendations begins with the following question: "Why?"

"Why?" opens the door to all manner of important follow-up questions such as, "What are you looking to achieve?" and "How are you envisioning that creating a [fill in the blank with the social media application du jour] account will help us to achieve this?"

More good advice: Begin with the *goal* as opposed to the *tool*. Many corporate communicators simply buckle under management's demands to start a blog or invade an existing social network to find out what customers are thinking. You would be best suited to ignore this pressure. Sometimes all it takes is a simple conversation that could go something like this:

Director of Marketing: "You mentioned you'd like the company to start tweeting. Are you familiar with Twitter?"
CEO: "No, but my daughter uses it and so do all of her friends."

Director of Marketing: "And what kind of business does she run?"

CEO: "I'm not sure I'm following you. She's 14 and in high school."

Director of Marketing: "No further questions. And no Twitter for you."

Okay, we were just having some fun with this example, but the takeaway is serious: If you suspect that your management team knows little about a tool they are demanding, stop to educate them on what the application is, how much it will cost in terms of staff resources, and how it might be used to meet a business objective. Also important to note is the distinction between personal use and corporate application. This cannot be overstated.

Education and awareness are more critical than ever in that well-intentioned requests from senior leaders who are unfamiliar with social media tactics can easily become very public mistakes. Now is not the time to "yes" your senior leadership because they're feeling left behind in the new media space. It is, however, a great opportunity to begin a dialogue in which objective, corporate commitment and resources can be addressed.

Don't let overly enthusiastic leadership steer you away from doing your job—a job that entails a clear focus on results and objectives, along with the best tools to help you get there. Know going in that you are planning to use a corporate blog as a tool for branding or a launching pad for lead generation. And know how you will measure the effects ahead of time.

The tricky part for many corporate marketers and communicators who are used to writing on behalf of senior leadership is that in the social media space, the rules of engagement change. If your

CFO wants to blog, check out her writing skills ahead of time. Is she personable? Can she devote the time to blog on a regular basis?

While you can certainly offer a few tweaks and suggestions, the key to effective blogs is establishing an authentic voice as opposed to an institutional mouthpiece. Bill Marriott is a stellar example of how one CEO took a liking to blogging and established a consistent voice and a message that resonates with his audience.[1]

As an advisor on matters of marketing and communications, you'll want to keep the sound judgment that's gotten you this far at the forefront of your decisions: Social media calls for an extra helping of rational thought leadership for maximum results.

If you are a company that has no distinct personality, consider social media as a means of creating one in line with your core values. Again, the key to social media is the "social" part—this means engaging audiences in a more personal and conversational way, while maintaining a level of professionalism.

You'll need to test a few strategies in a smaller pool before plunging into the sea. If you offer a call for social media assistance within your workplace only to realize that two of the five who raised their hands can't really write, and the other three, while well-intentioned, were simply too busy with their regular workload for an additional commitment, devise a Plan B.

Whether you are launching social media tools in response to eager management, or attempting to convince management of the importance of these tools, your goal should be to always start small. One giant leap that lands your company face first on the pavement will be a surefire way to secure your place *outside* of the social

---

[1] http://www.blogs.marriott.com/

media landscape. Better to gather up bite-sized successes that you can parlay into full-blown campaigns down the road.

Social media is far from free, so building an ongoing source of financial backing will be important as your efforts evolve. Some traps to avoid are the start-stop-start approach, where companies produce a few good blogs, get sidetracked during earnings season, go silent for a few months, then return to wonder where their audience has gone. Consistency is key, so commit before you start for best results.

Know who will participate going in: Will you have multiple tweeters on Twitter? Guest bloggers on your CEO's home page? Set the expectation up front and people will know where you're headed. Fail to tell them where you're going, make frequent and unplanned stops, and chances are your audience will choose a different mode of transportation to arrive at their informational destination.

In our experience, compulsory blogging and tweeting has yet to work effectively. If you have company buy-in, great. If you don't, rethink your strategy to match the organization's level of commitment. Some CEOs are more active than others—Tony Hsieh, former CEO of Zappos, is an outstanding case in point of a corporate executive who was highly engaged in the social media space. Quite simply, he got it and put it to work on behalf of the brand.[2]

Southwest Airlines is another company that gets it more than most when it comes to social media. In the case of Southwest, the airline clearly has an advocate in Christi Day, the company's specialist in emerging media, known to most as her Twitter handle

[2] http://blogs.zappos.com/blogs/ceo-and-coo-blog

(@Christi5321). Christi uses her bubbly personality to create personal engagement with followers and fans of the airline. But beyond her former-cheerleader persona, Day's underlying mission is to ensure that crises are snuffed out before they erupt through her prompt and targeted responses. This entails a great deal of monitoring of Southwest customers, followers and fans, which is part of her daily routine.

In fact, Southwest Airlines has become the poster child for doing social media right, from its "Nuts About You" blog, to its Flickr account that enables airplane watchers to finally have a place for all those great photos of airplane take-offs and landings, to its presence on Twitter. Legendary stories have emerged from Southwest's Twitter feed: from the minister stranded at an airport who tweeted his plight and found shelter for the night, to airplane delays and great deals on discount flights.

In early 2009, a Southwest flight attendant, David Holmes, was videotaped by a passenger on her cell phone as he rapped the otherwise deadly pre-flight safety instructions. The passenger told him she was going to post the clip to YouTube and he dared her to follow through. She did, and his rap was such a hit that it landed him on shows such as *Jay Leno* and *Late Night with David Letterman*.

Holmes followed this up by rapping at Southwest Airlines' annual shareholder meeting. The focus of this rap was the boilerplate statement on Generally Accepted Accounting Principles (GAAP)—aka the "GAAP Rap," which anyone who has had the pleasure of hearing them knows is an instant cure for insomnia. The rap was met with wild applause from shareholders.

Unlike many companies who have floundered in their social media endeavors, Southwest has seen a lot of sunshine in the social media space—and they'll need it.

A plane *will* crash, a flight *will* be delayed for an unacceptable period of time, and national-security or passenger-safety issues will arise. That's just a fact of the industry. But when a crisis does strike, Southwest can perhaps breathe just a little easier than other companies because it will have an ardent group of opinion leaders and influencers for support—in good times and in bad. This is where social media can really become a useful tool.

6

From Boot Camp to Base Camp:
Planning an Effective Mission

YOU'LL WANT TO PLAN your first social media venture like you plan any other marketing campaign, but with social media you will have access to deeper insights into your customers even before you launch. In fact, you'll need to gain an understanding of where your core audience is gathering before shaping your plan. The key is to develop parameters around your plan at the outset. Otherwise, you will find staff members consumed in a social media vortex—tweeting and posting their days away—with little to show for it.

The first thing you'll want to do is establish a benchmark of your core targets. The rule of smart people listening 90 percent of the time, and talking 10 percent of the time was never more apt than for those who are considering the launch of a social media plan. Conversation is king when it comes to social media, which equates to channels designed to prompt and facilitate conversations.

Like a cocktail party in which you spot an individual with whom you'd like to engage for the purposes of selling your product, you won't necessarily want to rush right in and launch into your pitch. You'll first want to stop and observe. You may look for an introduction from someone who knows the person you'd like to meet.

Or you might step into an existing conversation to better understand how you might add value—before delving into your primary reason for being there. The same is true with social media. Some questions to ask as you are shaping your plan:

• How will you find consumers on social networks?

• How will you migrate your existing consumer base onto active social networks to better engage with them? If they refuse to move, what can you bring to them via social networking?

• Where, when and how will you enter their conversations?

• What messages will your target group accept on their networks?

• Will you monitor their activity? If so, how and with what frequency?

• How will you create ongoing engagement once a relationship has been established?

This may seem like a lot to tackle, but you'll want to begin by monitoring activity to determine where your target groups are.

You can conduct this activity in a number of ways. Tools such as Search.Twitter.com, Yahoo Pipes—which enables users to aggregate content to meet their needs by creating and subscribing to unique "pipes" (e.g., dog lovers in Iowa, crafters, go-kart racing), Technorati for top blogs that your customers may be reading—or writing, or keyword searches across social media sites—all of which will begin to tell you where your audience may be.

Identifying your target is your first order of business. Do you know where you audience is? Are they reading blogs? Following your competitors on microblogs? Are they active in social networks? Posting to message boards? Are they subscribing to podcasts or RSS feeds? Are they tuned in to video blogs? Know this before entering the space and you won't be left wondering where your efforts to engage went wrong.

Once you have established a baseline of some of your most engaged customers or potential customers, you'll then want to turn to your staff to determine some suitable candidates for engaging on behalf of your company.

One simple way to round up your troops is to begin by identifying the heads of departments that your audience may most like to hear from. Determine whether they will represent the brand appropriately, whether their communication skills are appropriately honed, and their interest level in participating. Even those who are eager to blog on the top customer-service complaints—and offer solutions—must first be trained.

This begins with your social media policy (see Chapter 4). Many companies make the mistake of offering a policy full of "don'ts." The best social media policies are filled with "do's" along with rules of engagement, such as what's in scope and what's not from a content perspective (e.g., okay to talk about your personal plans to hold a yard sale over the weekend; not okay to reveal the upcoming roll-out of the company's long-awaited new release). Tone and style must also be a part of your policy and training so that employees know not only what to say, but how to say it in a manner that best represents your brand positioning.

Make no assumptions here, particularly because levels of formality can be subjective. If you want friendly and personable, but you don't want slang, jargon, or acronyms, say so up front so that all members of the company are clear on the expectations. Offer examples to showcase optimal tone and style.

Understanding the approach you will take—your strategy—is the next key step. This is where many companies inadvertently sabotage their own efforts. Many companies think they must enter the space with all cylinders firing, when in fact, the smarter approach is to choose just a couple of major social networking sites and begin to assess elements such as the amount of time it is taking staff to create and post content, and monitor its effects.

If your staff is feeling overwhelmed by updates to the company's Facebook page and weekly blog, then hold off on launching additional tools until they have become more acclimated to the routine—and until you are able to determine the return.

Of course, in addition to the engagement strategies you will create within your own social media accounts, you will also want to ensure that you are creating a presence in other people's networks as a means of creating a more pervasive presence in the online space. This can be as simple as offering comments on blogs that are relevant to your industry, or answering a question on LinkedIn within an interest group pertinent to your target market.

Thinking that your newly established Twitter account or your new social network on KickApps is going to draw psychic traffic to your site is another grave mistake that many companies have made. Like anything else, cross-channel promotion is a must if you are aiming for success.

FFor example, let's say you're in charge of marketing for Tall Moose Vodka. You've just launched your Tall Moose Twitter account and tweeted out a few great cocktail recipes. Next you're hosting a happy hour to kick off a new line of your vodka. Try strategies such as adding your Twitter account to the cocktail napkins—and depending on the savvy of the group, you may even add a mini Twitter tutorial and an incentive to sign on (e.g., "Tweet your favorite way to enjoy Tall Moose Vodka and win a 1.75 liter bottle. One prize awarded each day through June 30, 2010!")

The idea is to get your social media badges integrated into all of your marketing efforts so that these elements will start to gain traction. After all, what good is tweeting your message to an empty room?

Before you implement any of the above, you will also want to be certain that you know what you want out of all this—and what measures will deem this campaign a success. Know that it's not about quantity. Here, too, clients tell us their goals are "to have 10,000 fans on Facebook" or "5,000 Twitter followers by the end of the quarter." While we're not discounting the beauty of the masses, the more realistic and useful goal may be to focus more on quality engagements. Have you reached more or different people? Have you begun to get to know them: as opinion leaders, as supporters or as detractors of your brand? Have you enabled consumers to get to know your brand a bit better?

If your goal is to add some personality to your brand position-ing, are you seeing signs that this is happening? The measures of success in social media are different from traditional marketing measures, and often success and failure are in close proximity to one another. You may fail in gaining a significant following—or your contest may receive little response—but in the midst you may have stumbled upon a handful of voracious brand supporters who are delighted to be engaging with your brand in a more intimate way. Success.

With the above measures considered and reasonable expectations set, you are ready to create meaningful engagement with your stakeholders that will reposition your brand through the lens of the consumer voice. In an age in which peer-to-peer selling reigns supreme, this is precisely the direction you will want to take.

7

New to the Ranks of Social Media? Don't Get Psyched Out; Don't Get Cocky

FINDING A LESS-INSTITUTIONAL TONE—or even a great social media personality—can be a real trick for organizations. Some take to offering personal observations along with a dose of the brand message, as if they were having just another lunchroom conversation in the office. This can be both a good thing and a bad thing. Good thing: Social media works best with a measure of personality that indicates to consumers that there really are humans behind the brand. Bad thing: Social media fails to work when the personality falls out of alignment with the brand or overshadows it.

While social media has given marketing professionals and regular users of online media a chance to voice their opinions like never before, at times this has translated into a falling away from civil terms of engagement. Take Lance Armstrong and his Twitter slam against his Tour de France teammate, Alberto Contidor. In a world where personal branding counts, this wasn't necessarily a move we would recommend—particularly for a global sports icon.

Then there was the tweet from a now-former Ketchum VP in early 2009. The senior leader tweeted out this comment from his Twitter account the day before he was to meet with FedEx and present on digital media to the worldwide communications group in the company's hometown of Memphis:

> *True confession but I'm in one of those towns where I scratch my head and say, "I would die if I had to live here!"*[1]

Here's what the FedEx employees said in response:

> *Many of my peers and I feel this is inappropriate. We do not know the total millions of dollars FedEx Corporation pays Ketchum annually for the valuable and important work your company does for us around the globe. We are confident, however, it is enough to expect a greater level of respect and awareness from someone in your position as a vice president and a major global player in your industry. A hazard of social networking is people will read what you write. True confession: many of my peers and I don't see much relevance between your presentation this morning and the work we do in Employee Communications.*[2]

Aside from the obvious takeaway of, "Don't insult the client or the client's hometown," this is a cautionary tale that is not as far removed from us as we may think. In fact, we would all do well to take heed from the misstep that may easily have been ours in that the lines between public space and personal communication can

---

[1] http://twitter.com/keyinfluencer (January 14, 2009).
[2] http://www.davidhenderson.com/2009/01/21/key-online-influencer/

blur in an instant. Tweeting is publishing in a public space. Even if your competitors or your clients are not following you directly, this should never be an indication that you are alone in the room with colleagues and friends. Public space is public space. And the degrees of separation are few and getting fewer.

Most of the rules of new media aren't new at all. For instance, the rule of "just because you can, doesn't mean you should" seems apt. Social media empowers us with the ability to send out scathing reviews, personal attacks and unmitigated mudslinging commentaries in a matter of moments. But marketing and communications professionals know that these posts from celebrities, corporate leaders and irate employees become the core of image-makeover campaigns and are generally best avoided.

Social media gives us all the power to shape the future of the brands we represent—those that we love as consumers, and those that we think have not lived up to their value proposition and thus, have let us down. But with any power comes a measure of thinking through the consequences. While an irate diatribe against a top children's entertainment restaurant might feel great if the service was awful at your child's birthday party, the ripple effects of your rant might just outlive the anger you felt at the time.

Social media has a permanence unlike other media in that once your message is out there, taking it back becomes challenging at best, and impossible if it has really caught fire. So the best rule of thumb is to remember that the "s" in social media really does stand for "social": Creating a social engagement that entails a measure of civility, common sense, and playing by the same rules we all already know. Quite simply: Do the right thing, regardless of the medium, and you won't find yourself up at night sweating the aftermath of your 140-character mistake.

8

Know the Climate and Terrain

BETTER. FASTER. CHEAPER.

Many of us have been tasked with focusing on these areas regardless of our roles in the corporate setting. In fact, one company we worked with maintained a monthly Better, Faster, Cheaper (BFC) report, in which employees were mandated to offer an idea on how their department might enhance its BFCs in an ongoing way.

Social media can help you with the B, the F and the C—but only if you're smart in your approach, and understand how to navigate the terrain.

If senior leadership has demanded a full-throttle launch of social media, ask yourself first what the company is doing today. If you are charged with bringing a social media campaign to life, treat it as you would any other assignment, but in this case, you'll have to consider some additional elements such as the ground rules to accompany your company's objectives.

Organizations such as the Wisconsin-based Snap-on Inc. have close to 25,000 fans on Facebook, where avid tool aficionados who have become fans of the company's page are able to contribute photos, videos and their comments on Snap-on's products.

Alicia Smales, the spokesperson for Snap-on, maker of hand and power tools, and in business since 1920 when it was known as the Snap-On Wrench Company, notes that the company's Facebook page "allows us to swiftly communicate with Snap-on enthusiasts of all ages. Snap-on fans are actively sharing their stories and their experiences with Snap-on. It's really amazing to see how engaged (they) are and how enthusiastically they interact with each other."[1]

The above is a great example of how companies can reinvent themselves and reengage consumers based on understanding where they are and what their customers need.

Another question to ask as you consider your potential engagement points is whether your company runs the risk of disseminating key company information via social media such as trade secrets, or proprietary or investor relations information that could be crucial to a company's success and devastating should it be released. Remember that while the rules of engagement may be different, your legal team should be brought in early in the process to ensure that problems don't develop down the road. Being faster is never better when it means violating SEC rules or inviting shareholder concern.

Bearing in mind that social media began not as a handy set of marketing tools, but as a means for people to socialize with other people, when companies attempt to infiltrate a social space, they must do so by listening first, being transparent about who they

---

[1] Press release found at: www1.snapon.com/display/231/ToolNews/.../2009/Facebook15000.pdf
Snap-on Tools Facebook page can be found at: http://www.facebook.com/SnaponTools

represent, asking permission, treating customers with respect, and offering value in terms of interest and engagement.

Once you have determined that your audience—or at least an attractive or sizeable enough segment—is in the social media space, your next job is to determine where your employees are in relation to your customers and your brand.

In an ideal world, employees are your brand ambassadors and should be expected to represent your brand across all public spaces, both on and off the job. And yet, humans that they are, employees get frustrated or mad, find themselves passed over for promotions, or simply clash with coworkers—and they tend to vent to friends and family. Chances are we have all done this at some point in our careers. The problem isn't the content, it's the context.

When friends and family migrate into a public space for their personal conversations, the dynamics change significantly. Suddenly, how your employees talk about your brand on their personal Facebook page becomes your concern—and as we have noted, should become a part of your company's social media policy. Not only *what* they post but *when* can become problematic for the brand.

For example, if you have an employee who is tweeting in a personal capacity about the company for which he or she works between the hours of 9 a.m. and 5 p.m., this could easily become fodder for lax policies at your organization, or the starter tweet for an article about the rise in disgruntled employees within your firm. Neither of these is the phone call you want to answer from the media.

Therefore, it becomes important to create education and awareness amongst employees at the outset so that they know what is in bounds and what is out. This conversation should always take place within the context of your social media policy.

Even if your company isn't ready to launch anything beyond an e-newsletter, it's smart to have a policy for employees. Keep in mind it's not just your content and channels you are concerned with; it's what your employees are saying in their personal space. Much of this may seem harmless to staff members who may be used to sharing gripes about the boss or the workload with friends. But when the friends turn up on public spaces, this immediately places your brand in a position of risk.

Sometimes all it takes is an understanding of the connection between the personal MySpace page and references to your brand, because employees simply haven't thought about the implications. In other cases, you may need to step in to request a cease and desist from a rogue employee who may be inappropriately representing the corporate image.

While you may be thinking this type of activity is confined to the office worker, consider this: In October 2009, in the midst of the NFL season, Kansas City Chiefs' running back, Larry Johnson, tweeted offensive comments about head coach Todd Haley after a game against San Diego in which the Chiefs were routed 37-7. Johnson tweeted from an alias account name "Toonicon," which links to his personal website, so the connection was not hard to uncover. Since the incident, Johnson's Twitter account has been made private, but the story—and its ripple effect on the player, himself—lives on as part of the larger question of personal and professional use of social media applications.[2]

---

[2] http://sports.espn.go.com/nfl/news/story?id=4596288 (October 27, 2009).

Thus, it is worth careful consideration of all sides—that is, of all of your potential content creators and all of your potential audiences—when it comes to managing your brand.

The most widely cited case of an organization that really knew and understood its content creators and audiences was the 2008 Obama presidential campaign committee. While you likely have read about or witnessed firsthand the 2008 presidential campaign with regard to social media, we will recount it again here as a primer on social media effectiveness and as a pivotal case study that anyone considering social media tactics should be familiar with.

Despite some reports, both John McCain and Barack Obama had a social media presence, but the differences in online impact were dramatic. We'll begin with a recap of results: From the conventions through to the November 2008 elections, as noted in a study compiled by Trendrr (November 5, 2008), overall blog mentions of Obama were 500 million, compared to McCain's 150 million. Obama's MySpace Friends were 844,927, to McCain's 219,404. Likewise, on Twitter, Obama followers were118,107 to McCain's 4,942.[3]

In fact, Obama's online presence significantly outpaced the McCain campaign in every online space—from YouTube, to campaign web pages in the Google index, to Flickr and more. Obama's advantage was that the demographic of those engaged in social media tended to fall directly in line with current Democratic voters. Hence, Obama's campaign held the distinct advantage of having content creators perfectly positioned to push forth a message en masse in a viral way.

---

[3] Frederic Lardinois, "Obama's Social Media Advantage" (November, 2008).
http://www.readwriteweb.com/archives/social_media_obama_mccain_comparison.php

Obama's campaign was far more active, far savvier and far more comfortable in the social media space. The Obama campaign mobilized its grassroots support via social media tactics such as mobile text and e-mail (via opt-in text messages); YouTube and other video sharing sites; effective use of its supporter database; maintaining a presence where users were; and empowering and enabling the community to move beyond that space through active participation with events, rallies or phone banks. To restate this point: The beauty of the Obama social media campaign was its ability to move users *beyond* the social media space and out into the real world.

While it is important to note that the Obama campaign had at its disposal an astounding budget for new media, somewhere in the neighborhood of $78 million (so don't be discouraged if you are attempting a similar campaign on a budget of, say, $100,000— or $5,000—and wondering why your results don't look quite the same), still the campaign enacted smart and cost-effective media buys. The total amount spent on Facebook was $467,000, but Obama's Facebook presence is estimated to have generated as much buzz, and as many donations and votes as the rest of his ad spending combined (hundreds of millions of dollars).

The objective of the Obama campaign was to raise money, awareness and supporters. According to The Washington Post, in his 21-month campaign, Obama raised more than $500 million through online contributions.[4] In addition, he gathered a list of 13 million e-mail addresses, and his aides sent 7,000 different e-mails, segmented and targeted at different levels of donors, for a total of 1 billion e-mails sent.[5] In addition, one million people signed up for

---

[4] Jose Antonio Vargas, "Obama Raised Half a Billion Online," (Washington Post, November 20, 2008). http://voices.washingtonpost.com/44/2008/11/20/obama_raised_half_a_billion_on.html
[5] Ibid.

Obama's text-message program, in which supporters received five to 20 text messages per month depending on where they lived and the kinds of messages they opted to receive (segmented by states, regions, zip codes and colleges).

Obama's outreach included his own social network, but in addition, two million profiles were created; 200,000 offline events planned; 400,000 blog posts written; and 35,000 volunteer groups created. On user-generated MyBarackObama (MyBO) fundraising pages, 70,000 people raised $30 million, and supporters were trained to collect small-dollar donations from friends, relatives and coworkers.

But the Obama campaign made great use of other people's networks (OPNs) as well, garnering 6 million followers on Facebook, nearly 500,000 followers on Twitter and roughly 5 million supporters on other social networks. He maintained profiles in 15 online communities, and his Facebook supporters created a popular group called Students for Barack Obama, a group that was so effective that senior aides made it an official part of the campaign.

A total of 5.4 million Facebook users clicked on an "I Voted" button to let Facebook friends know that they went to the polls, thus we see a flawless execution of online peer pressure. But long before the presidential campaign was over, the Obama campaign was already planning the post-election campaign. Obama's transition site was launched two days after he was elected. Addresses were videotaped and archived on YouTube, and an e-mail with the subject line: "Where do we go from here?" offered a detailed survey asking supporters for input on moving forward, and requesting community volunteers. Obama for America (OFA) became Organizing for America (OFA2.0) to continue to harness grassroots efforts. Interestingly, and perhaps problematically, OFA2.0 is run through the Democratic National Committee (DNC), and has already begun developing plans for the 2012 re-election campaign. In fact, the annual budget for OFA2.0 is a whopping $75 million.[6]

Regardless of which side of the political house you are sitting on, the Obama presidential campaign marks an unprecedented example of the power of social media to affect online and offline activity.

---

[6] M.J. Piskorski and L. Winig, "Barack Obama: Organizing for America 2.0," HBS No. 9-709-493 (Boston, Harvard Business School Publishing, April 4, 2009).

9

Build a Social Media Shelter

I F YOUR COMPANY has been experimenting or is actively engaged with social media, you may have experienced an unexpected phenomenon: Several Twitter accounts, a Facebook account for each of five sub-brands, two LinkedIn sites, a few web portals and of course, a system or two such as HootSuite or TweetDeck for managing the daily activity with these applications. This network of accounts can leave you with a sinking feeling that if you lost all the scraps of paper with the various pieces of information, your social media efforts would be lost.

What's worse, you're not sure which e-mail address goes with which account since your project leader set up the accounts as a convenience to you. Not so convenient when the project manager leaves in short order, taking her intimate knowledge of your accounts with her. That's why you'll need to create a social media shelter in the form of managing your multiple social media accounts.

Three points will give you peace of mind:

1. CREATE A PLAN FOR CREATING ACCOUNTS

Multiple accounts within one application often require discreet e-mail addresses, so you'll want to consider your plan for e-mail account creation for the purposes of social media, along with whether you will have—or need to have—multiple accounts within one social network, and the optimal naming convention.

For example, will you launch just one main branded Twitter account? Or, will separate regional accounts work more effectively on behalf of your brand? If you are a national bookseller wanting to drive traffic for author book signings, a national Twitter account alone may be insufficient, as customers in Georgia don't care about the book signing in the San Fernando Valley next Wednesday night. In this case @booksSFV, @booksNY, and @booksGA may be the way to go to really become useful and effective at the local level.

Corporate addresses are centrally important in that companies are finding that one employee using multiple existing work and personal e-mail addresses can muddy the waters when he or she moves on, causing accounts to become dormant or inaccessible.

The best advice is to plan for company-based accounts that multiple users and administrators can access without compromising individual, personal security.

2. DETERMINE YOUR POLICY FOR ASSOCIATING INDIVIDUAL INFORMATION WITH ACCOUNT PROFILES

If, for instance, you are creating a Facebook account for Rob's Running Shoes, you will find it preferable to create a business account as opposed to an individual user account, or even a Facebook group administered by Mary Smith, your weekend clerk—who is leaving for college at the end of the summer. If the Facebook account is linked to Mary Smith, then Mary Smith is forever linked to Rob's Running Shoes or, if Mary has had enough of athletic footwear, a new account will need to be created. So, you can see where this is headed: A break in the stream, market confusion over why current sites have gone silent, etc. These are situations you must avoid through foresight and planning at the account setup stage.

3. ORGANIZE YOUR ACCOUNTS

A simple Excel spreadsheet can work wonders in taking disparate account information and creating a handy reference to be shared amongst core users. Listing site name, e-mail address, username and password for each of your multiple accounts will save time and put a stop to the confusion factor when it comes to managing sites. You can also invest in a system to manage your passwords, such as Password Manager Pro, which will store your passwords securely in one centralized location.

If you've ever stopped to ask yourself, "Did I create that Flickr account using myname@thismail.com or myname@thatmail. com?" or "Is my password for the Veggie Lovers' YouTube channel 'veggie123' or '123veggie?'," you will appreciate the upfront planning in what will likely become your ever-growing collection of social media accounts.

10

Recruit Your Troops

I F YOU ARE HEADING communications, marketing, or public relations efforts in some capacity, you will likely have to recruit people from within your organization who are interested in social media. If you can elicit support from senior leadership within your organization, let the people with the passion for the job run with it.

Why? They'll be more likely to make the time. They'll have fun doing it. They'll feel more empowered. And ideally, they will forge relationships with your key constituents who will, in turn, become your strongest allies in times of celebration—and, perhaps more importantly, crisis.

Before you spend all your energies on a social media love affair, only to feel like a jilted lover when the response proves lukewarm at best, consider the following: Patience is a virtue with direct carryover into the social media space. If you are planning for a groundswell of followers akin to the handful of videos and marketing campaigns that have truly "gone viral," reconsider your expectations. For starters, you may not need a mass, viral following to meet your objective. Instead, you may need a small but dedicated core to get the job done.

Social media is time-consuming work, and unless you're able to give up attending meetings, networking with colleagues, presenting strategy, and implementing tactics both in and out of the social media space, you're going to need that backup.

The speed at which social media applications can be started is disarming—*and has nothing to do with the pace at which you will see results.* While it takes less than five minutes to create a new Twitter account and send your first tweet, it may take many, many months to establish a following—and even then, your Twitter following might look more like a smattering of birds on a clothesline than a flock of hungry seagulls at a beach barbecue.

Along with buying into the myth that rapid account setup equals rapid fan and follower acquisition, positioning yourself as an "expert" in the social media space within your company is also unwise. If you are charged with establishing a social media campaign, be upfront with what you know and what you don't. And if you have vendors who tell you *they* are experts, look elsewhere. The reality is that the tools and metrics are too new and are being applied with dramatically different controls (e.g., massive budgets, no budget at all; teams of content creators or the lone blogger).

Thus, the best advice for today's professional charged with spearheading a social media campaign is to become a social media student and to educate those around you along the way. This iterative process of sharing best practices, learning from mistakes and strengthening our collective social media intelligence will be the real keys to success with new media.

PART II
Expedient Content Starters

WITH SO MANY TOOLS and applications and metrics at our disposal, one might feel stopped at, "Where to begin?" This section outlines some of your best bets for generating content designed to move your audience to active engagement. Of note is that these do not appear in any priority ranking, simply because we don't know where the bulk of your audience resides, so determining the "best places" to employ will be a question that you will need to ask yourself as you read through some of the tactics to determine those that will best optimize your abilities to engage.

11

Content, Community, Commerce

BECAUSE OF ITS EXTREME IMPORTANCE, we'll start with the takeaway from this chapter: First and foremost, and above all else as you are shaping your marketing and communications strategy, your content—whether it is links or photos, or video or a shareholders' report—must be socially enabled.

To state this another way: If your content isn't equipped for the RSS-share-save-post-to revolution, then don't even bother. Period.

It is no longer sufficient to simply create content and hope that visitors will come to you. So, for instance, while blogging "gets you out there," Real Simple Syndication (RSS) "gets you out there" even more. Real Simple Syndication is, in essence, a family of web feed formats used to publish frequently updated content such as blog entries, news headlines, podcasts and more. Your goal for any content you create is simple: Syndication. That is, you will want to create it once, then make it available to be published in multiple places. On the consumer end, you will want to do all that you can to maximize subscribers—those who have signed on to receive your RSS feed—because more subscribers equals more consumers.

As for what content can do for you in the first place, we now return to our regularly scheduled chapter. Your content positions you as an expert or a go-to place to solve prospects' problems. Whether you are a media outlet, a major brand or an entrepreneur, your goal is to serve as a trusted source of information and advice that is relevant to your target audience.

In a world that has lost confidence in government, news media (perceived bias), financial markets and the global economy, you and your site must be seen as trusted advisors. And everyone must carve out a niche of expertise. On the social media playing field, no one is exempt.

One way to create content is to organize and share your company's "favorites" (e.g., most-popular brands, best value, funniest of the year, etc.).

Just as social networks organize people with like interests and enable sharing amongst them, social bookmarking services enable an organization to share content with consumers (e.g., sites, pages, articles, blog posts).

Social bookmarking, which is a cloud-computing application, has become a great means of audience engagement. Whereas in Web 1.0, a user might add an interesting site as a bookmark or favorite, this action was tied to one computer. In Web 2.0, social bookmarks are virtual bookmarks. They go where the user goes and thus, have greater reach for enabling other users to discover what's new and what's popular—ideally centered on your brand.

Social news and bookmarking sites allow web users to save, organize and share their bookmarks of web pages on the Internet (versus their own computers). Social news sites allow users to submit web pages and articles and have other users vote on them with the number of votes determining which articles are presented on the social news site. This is good news for your brand in that it broadens the scope of opportunity in terms of reaching target groups and staying top of mind for consumers.

Some of the top social bookmarking sites for this include Delicious.com, one of the first virtual bookmarking services, along with Digg.com, Reddit.com and StumbleUpon.com. Your brand's collection of social bookmarks tells consumers who you are, your understanding of their interests and needs, and your expertise. As a marketer charged with promoting a brand in this space, you will want to be positioned as a go-to aggregator on a topic (e.g., handbags, golf clubs, tax preparation and so forth).

Creating a corporate wiki, a collaborative website that allows users to contribute to and edit the content on the website, may be another option within your content strategy. Wikipedia is perhaps the most famously known wiki, but there are countless wikis in the online space, which can offer unique and valuable informa-tion. If you're not sure where to begin with a wiki, Wikifarms hosts multiple wikis and provides tools for users to create their own wikis. Increasing numbers of businesses are creating wikis to allow their customers to interact with one another and with them (e.g., Wetpaint, Wikia).

On the video front, while YouTube was once the place to go for off-beat, user-generated content, it has expanded into premium content because in the face of always-lurking competition, it wants to be the go-to place for all video—so you'll want to be there as well if you are able. We'll talk in depth about the corporate use of video in Chapter 16.

Ultimately, your goal must be to produce or aggregate compelling content as the core of your successful online strategy. Create a marketplace of ideas and if the content is good, consumers will share. Thus, it is important to enable social bookmarking around your content via plug-ins (e.g., "share" tools such as "ShareThis") featuring a range of applications through which consumers can share your brand's content.

While content is forever king, traffic is the emperor online. Consider this as "online existentialism": If no one knows you're there, you don't exist. You'll want to carefully consider distribution of your content, and your company's potential to grab audience share. Whereas consumer product goods companies buy limited shelf space in retail outlets, in the digital space the shelf space is endless. So, to consider traffic another way—it's a bad thing when you're sitting in your car on the freeway—but it's the only thing when your site is sitting in the middle of the Web desert.

Your strategy must be based on the three Cs: Content, community and commerce. The content will attract visitors to your online sites through relevant, current, compelling information. Once users arrive for your content, you must optimize your opportunity by creating an immediate sense of community. You will want to engage your visitors, retain their interest, and give them reasons to remain active, explore further, and return to your community. Finally, you'll want to pay attention to commerce by developing ways to monetize your visitors (e.g., advertising revenue, subscription fees, e-commerce purchases, lead generation).

This also includes your sub-domain strategy [e.g., SEO, Google (earth.google.com), HowStuffWorks, CraigsList, etc.]. You will want to own more "eye space" on Google results than your competitors in that space. To this end, one sound strategy is to start more sites about your own business and more links back and forth from site to site. Set up a Wikipedia business page and an AboutUs.org page—both of which should be heavily linked to your other sites. You will want to explore setting up profiles on social networks such as Facebook, MySpace, LinkedIn and Yahoo. And with tools such as Squidoo, for instance, you can position your company as an expert via articles.

No matter what level of content you produce, you will want to leverage it. Your mantra must be:

"Create it once. Publish it in multiple places and in multiple media forms."

Your strategy for content reach must travel online and off in order to increase your effectiveness with content syndication and ultimately, media consumption. So it may likely include such items as blogs, podcasts, MP3 audio files, hard-copy CDs, RSS distribution, e-books, print books, and seminars (note that we've mixed online and offline distribution). To get this right, marketers must focus not on how *they* like to consume content, but rather on how *their audiences* may want to consume content. This entails making your content available in a wide range of formats to meet all potential consumers' media consumption preferences. If you don't meet these needs, you will be missing opportunities. Create content for readers (e.g., books, e-books, blogs), listeners (podcasts, CDs—enabling multitasking), watchers (video), expe-riencers (face-to-face events) and interacters (digital, user-gener-ated storytelling).

Worth attention is identifying groups of consumers based on levels of engagement as outlined by Forrester Research: Creators—Publish, upload content; Critics—Post comments, ratings, edit wikis; Collectors—Save URLs, tags, vote on social bookmarking sites; Joiners—Maintain profiles, participate in social networking sites; Spectators—Consume what others produce; Inactives— Online, but not engaged.[1]

The appeal of the "triple-C" sites is that they blend content, community and commerce to create a compelling user experience. The majority of sites today employ this strategy, at least to some degree. Users can communicate with one another through social media functionality, and can decide for themselves which content they would prefer to consume. They can create their own content (e.g., ratings, reviews, recommendations, other commentary, video/photo uploads), or participate in commerce related to the context of the community in which they are participating.

The triple-C objective is simple. If you are going to spend the resources to drive visitors to your site, you must create a good user/customer experience, and keep users engaged, which will, in turn, increase monetization opportunities, get them to come back for more, and get them to tell others. Start the conversation where your audience is already sharing information and influencing peers within a group. Stepwise, you must find the fish—swim in the pool with the fish you need, or aggregate pools of consumers; keep the fish swimming (e.g., open up to third-party applications or Other People's Functionality (OPFs) such as Facebook); stir up the waters (e.g., add ongoing "content bait" allowing users to participate by commenting, rating and creating); and let the fish attract more fish. Grow the network virally to increase ad inventory and thus monetization opportunities.

---

[1] Forrester's North American Social Technographics Survey, (Q2 2007).

Important to remember is that media consumption and creation is now in the hands of the consumer. Web and other technologies (wireless devices) enable users to pick and choose and to surround themselves with the content they want. Your job as a marketer is to enable "experience personalization" to retain users through widgetized homepages (e.g., Netvibes and iGoogle), desktop gadgets and eardrums (audio playlists).

You will want to seek out forms of content consumption that exist in your company's arsenal (e.g., traditional media such as television, magazines, radio—or even other types of Web 1.0 websites) that don't provide interactivity and personalization, and replace them with Web 2.0 components.

The content "bait" you will use can be anything—and everything—from news such as text stories, photos or videos. You'll want these to be factual elements, not editorial pieces used to seed discussions on social sites and generate user commentary. Entertainment content, such as celebrity news and gossip is another great conversation starter, as is political content, which is naturally controversial and thus, a good starting point for lively debate.

Social media enables users to discover, explore and get at the truth (e.g., ratings, recommendations, related articles). Here is where collaboration between traditional media (facts) and bloggers (mix of facts and opinions) becomes critical in that consumers need to flesh out the "truth" and thus, fill in the gaps. The Wisdom of Crowds is in full swing in the Web 2.0 world. No longer will it suffice to trust one source (especially if it's the advertiser). Rather, there is strength (credibility) in numbers. These "crowds" are then used to create and organize content (e.g., social bookmarking aggregators such as Delicious and Digg).

You will also want to choose the online business model that best suits your objective—and you'll want to move beyond the advertising model (e.g., Google, portals, newspapers). Models to consider are subscription (e.g., Wall Street Journal Online, application service providers such as Salesforce.com), the e-Commerce model (buying and selling product), the affiliate model (selling other people's product), and the lead-generation model (selling leads). If you are charged with marketing via social media, you must keep an eye on diversification beyond the strict ad model.

Two more Cs for content creation are clarity and credibility. Clarity means you must eliminate the clutter, create sufficient white space, offer simple navigation and quickly be able to answer the question on behalf of your customers of, "What's in it for me?" Your credibility will be built on a professional look, avoiding freeware that comes with ads, including trust badges that offer a halo effect (e.g., borrowing clients' or associated providers' credibility) and featuring client logos if you are a service provider.

Based on Google eye-tracking studies, we know that people perform quick scans on websites—generally in the upper-left and down-left navigation. This type of insight can help when designing an optimized landing page. Don't focus resources on acquiring traffic without spending time on capturing attention and converting browsers to buyers. Begin with good design basics, but let no one but your customers—not even your professional web design team—tell you what your site should ultimately look like. Test via Constant and Never-Ending Improvement (CANI) to maximize your conversions. Test radically different versions of your site, and then hone these based on iterative results.

You'll also want to aggregate content through niche sites—or niche channels within these sites. Again, your goal is to position your brand as the "go-to" place. Fight against media fragmentation by offering choice to consumers, and by doing away with the need for visitors to go anywhere else. Most people aren't going to remember or take the time to type in your URL. They will discover you—perhaps from your content embedded in a widget that links back to your site. RSS technology enables syndication of your "headlines" which then link back to your site.

To this end, you may want to consider the services of a content curator or syndicator as a means of adding depth to your bench. Syndicators aggregate content by licensing it from content providers (e.g., Associate Press, Getty Images, newspapers, magazines, broadcasters). These are paid/reseller or ad revenue share models. Web publishers can then obtain feeds or clips of stories, images or video related to topics on your site. Such content aggregators include: Daylife, Mochila, ClipSyndicate, JamboTV and Voxant.

In a social media framework, the content-driven brands will succeed. You will want to be one of these.

12

Catching Social Butterflies?
Find the Right Net

S O, WHERE ARE THEY? Your audience, that is. Are they out walking in the park most afternoons, without even so much as a cell phone? Are they technology lovers, who never leave home without their iPhone or BlackBerry as they head outdoors with the latest bestseller downloaded on their portable, wireless reader? This is an important question that many people fail to ask.

There are several ways to tell whether your audience will be receptive to your advances in social media. Demographics such as age, ethnicity and gender are certainly some good measures. But these should never be the sole driving force behind your campaign.

We talked about the importance of providing strong content in syndicated ways, and here we'll discuss some of the core tools you will want to consider based on your initial research into your customer base. To offer some context as to why these distribution points are important, keep in mind that your goal should never be the social media tactic, itself. For example, gathering 50,000 users to a Flickr account without knowing why is equivalent to inviting top dignitaries to a meeting place—having them all miraculously show up for your event—and then realizing you hadn't stopped to consider what you would do with them once you got them there.

The retail industry sheds light on the value of some of the tools you may want to consider. In fact, many retailers are using social media to engage customers in deeper ways in areas such customer service (Zappos), new product ideas ("My Starbucks Idea" blog) and product reviews (Target, Walmart).

Know that what happens online does not stay online—and this is precisely what we are aiming for. Social media marketing efforts are premised on turning consumers of information into brand advocates across all media channels.

Using the retail industry as an example, we know that brick-and-mortar stores continue to dominate the market, but the influences that drive consumers to active on-ground shopping—and keep them coming back and engaged—can be attributable to activities within the social media space.

According to an article by the Nielsen Company (Swedowsky, 2009), traffic to shopping web sites skyrocketed as Black Friday 2009 approached. Consumers looking to educate themselves on the best bargains spent more and more time online doing research so they would be prepared to make the best in-store purchases on the Friday after Thanksgiving. "Week-over-week, traffic to these sites has increased 87 percent, from 3.8 million unique visitors during the week ending Nov. 8 to 7.0 million during the week ending Nov. 15,"[1] leading the retail industry to surmise that

---

[1] Maya Swedowsky, "Consumers Rush the Web Early for Black Friday Deals," (Nielson Wire, November 25, 2009). http://blog.nielsen.com/nielsenwire/consumer/consumers-rush-the-web-early-for-black-friday-deals/

online activity is having an influence over offline behaviors. Like the Obama campaign, in which volunteers received text messages and personalized e-mails—which translated into active, grassroots efforts, this is precisely the effect we as marketers are looking to achieve.

While direct causality is never an easy case to make, across industries research is pointing to distinct upticks in online activities, which can be correlated to offline activities. For example, across the board, social media sites are becoming more mainstreamed. User-generated content is added to the Web 2.0 space in a 24/7 cycle. Traffic to Facebook, Twitter and LinkedIn have seen wild increases in the past year alone. Not only are people visiting these social networking sites, but they are spending more time in these spaces than ever before.

Peer-to-peer advocacy is in full swing. Now, instead of asking a core of friends and family for their thoughts on a product they are considering, consumers can ask a world of consumers for their thoughts, opinions, experiences and advice. And this is more powerful than any ad could hope to be. Now, in addition to formal surveys, focus groups and voter polls, companies can listen to natural, peer-to-peer conversation for a more raw and unbiased glimpse into how consumers are feeling about particular brands, products or services.

We are often asked if social media "listening" should replace all other forms of customer feedback, and the answer to this is no. Social media should serve in a complementary fashion to validate or refute traditional survey and focus group results. Social media tactics will enable you to sketch an ongoing, real-time picture of your brand: how consumers are feeling about it, and if they are even thinking about it at all. In addition, social media lets you surface potential customer service concerns before they become unwieldy. And it can help companies to monitor their reputations to spot potential issues and identify opportunities for stronger brand positioning.

ON BECOMING SOCIAL

Social networking services—Facebook and MySpace being two of the most well-known, though depending on the region of the world in which you live, you may know hi5, Bebo, Orkut or Sonico as your network of choice—are websites that allow online users to connect and share information with other online users. More and more companies are leveraging social networks to promote their brands and services and to connect with customers and potential customers. Other do-it-yourself social networking sites include KickApps and Ning.

In January 2009, the Pew Internet and American Life Project presented these statistics[2]:

• Adult Internet users who have a profile on an online social network rose from 8% in 2005 to 35% in 2009

• 75% of adults 18-24 have at least one social network profile versus 7% of adults 65 and older

• Across all age groups, social networks are used more heavily for personal than professional purposes

[2] Sydney Jones & Susannah Fox, "Pew Internet Project Demo," (January 28, 2009). http://pewinternet.com/

• Adults and teens use social networking sites to connect with people they already know

MORE THAN JUST A PRETTY FACEBOOK

Beginning with people searching out people they know, we start with Facebook. Facebook continues to attract users at a skyrocketing rate. Facebook was launched by computer science students at Harvard in 2003 and in less than one month, half of the undergraduate population had signed on to the service. In 2009, Facebook claims to have more than 60 million active members and has averaged 250,000 new registrations every day since the beginning of 2007. More than half of its users return every day, generating more than 65 billion page views each month. The Facebook site notes an 85 percent market share of four-year universities, and as of June 2008, visitor growth was up 152 percent annually (as opposed to 3 percent for MySpace).

Businesses are taking advantage of Facebook's population density by creating pages of their own designed to capture existing traffic to the site. For example, Visa uses Facebook to its advantage via The Visa Business Network Facebook page designed to connect small business owners with one another, and to help them in promoting their businesses to a larger community. Burger King garnered a bit of infamy for itself when it launched its "Whopper sacrifice" on Facebook in which users were asked to delete 10 friends in exchange for a coupon good for one free Whopper. A whopping 20,000 users quickly signed on, but the promotion was shut down shortly thereafter due to privacy concerns.

Ultimately, the goal of social media is to help companies to position themselves to be discovered by core consumer groups. This can occur via blogs, social media networks and search engine optimization strategies. The problem for many companies is that they stop at counting numbers of Facebook fans, or Twitter followers and call this "success."

In fact, the next step after being discovered by customers or potential customers is engaging them through establishing connections via your Facebook page, website, landing page, or e-mail capture, thus turning passers-by into leads, customers and sales. Only then can you call social media marketing efforts successful in quantifiable measure. And you will want to analyze your results in an ongoing fashion—in light of your company's objectives, your competitors and evolving consumer trends.

Facebook can provide small businesses with a cost-effective means of positioning themselves and reaching target groups with the potential for high return. Like everything else in social media, success is not necessarily based on quantity. Most Facebook pages have less than 500 fans.

If your company is new to Facebook, you will want to establish a business account and fill out a complete profile. Nothing says consumer uncertainty faster than an incomplete profile. When it comes to Facebook's policies for business accounts, the best advice is to read through their policies carefully for the most up-to-date information to ensure against any glitches based simply on a lack of understanding of the Facebook rules.

You will want to consider carefully whether your Facebook account updates will feed into your company's Twitter account, or vice versa (generally the former is preferred, as constant tweets poured into the Facebook platform can become pesky). As with setting up all corporate social media accounts, be sure to make public only those parts of the corporate profile that you are comfortable having the public see.

If you will showcase an individual—or if your brand is an individual—choose a photo that best aligns with the brand's overall image (e.g., is your brand laid-back and casual in the eyes of its consumers? If so, then pass on the image of the CEO in suit and tie, and go for the photo from the company's picnic). If you don't have exactly what you need to align leadership with the brand, it's worth the cost of a photo session to capture the precise image. You will ideally use this image in multiple spaces, so you'll get a lot of mileage from it.

If you have "evergreen" information that you'd like each and every fan to have access to, be sure to place links to your main website, product offering or free-sample invitation as built-in content within your company's profile.

While getting your own Facebook presence in order is essential, be sure to go out and meet the neighbors as well. Join interest and industry groups, comment on their walls and offer information of value.

Promote your Facebook presence across all marketing materials—from your standard business card, to your e-mail signature, to brochures, mailers, leave-behinds, video segments and of course, your key website(s). The goal is always to give your audiences additional ways to engage with your brand.

Many companies do a fine job of establishing their Facebook presence, but then fall down at knowing what to offer as ongoing content. You'll want to think this through carefully before setting up shop. The key is perceived value. Sharing links to video of a conference your company attended, or an update on product development or interesting company activities are all good choices. The key is to keep customers and prospective customers interested and wanting to come back.

Other means of engagement include Facebook-only discounts or special offers, demonstrating community by asking industry experts to share content via a guest article, and answering consumers' questions in a manner that is timely and conveys a willingness to respond and forge relationships. Be sure to research those who have become a friend or fan, and determine if their friends or fans may be of interest to you. Also check out your competitors for their Facebook activities and to determine the types of fans that are following them—and how you might engage these individuals as well.

If you have industry data that you are legally able to share, this can be a great way of offering consumers an inside look at a topic of interest to them. Look for connections you might be able to forge as a facilitator. For example, if you are asked for a solution that your company doesn't provide, but you are able to connect a prospective customer with a colleague who can assist, this is a win for the brand.

While it will cost your company nothing to establish a Facebook presence, you will likely want to include Facebook's social ads to your repertoire for a more targeted approach.

In essence, the principle behind Facebook ads, around only since 2007, is that they are targeted toward individuals who would find the ad most relevant and interesting—and then passed on to their network of friends who might also find them relevant and interesting, with the added benefit of coming with a peer "endorsement" of sorts. In essence, Facebook employs an algorithm that turns Facebook users into laser-focused marketing allies because they deliver your message to their closest friends.

Keep in mind that people flock to Facebook not to meet people, but to reconnect with people they know and to see what their friends are doing and what they like. Thus, the endorsements that appear on a friend's page become more of a peer-mediated soft sell, which advertisers hope will translate into positive return.

If you are considering Facebook for your company's brand image, you will want to create not just a business account, but either a group or a fan page—more likely both—as each can offer distinct advantages. The fan page and the group share many common features such as hosting discussions, messaging all members and accommodating video and photo exchange.

Fan pages enjoy the advantage of visibility to those who are unregistered in Facebook, but their number one advantage is getting your company indexed for optimal search engine positioning. Fan pages that have met with great success include adidas, Red Bull and Pringles. To create a fan page, visit facebook.com/pages/create.php and follow the steps to create a new page.

On the other hand, creating a group allows you to send out mass appeals (invitations, special offers). To create a group, visit facebook.com/groups/create.php and complete the form for the type of group (e.g., open or closed, such as an alumni-only group). Groups will have an administrator who may approve applicants or recruit members via an "invitation-only" approach.

Ultimately, groups are ideal for more acute interactions that involve a particular cause or action, whereas pages are best for brands wishing to create a long-term relationship that is not tied to an individual administrator.

Experimentation continues to drive new trends in Facebook marketing. One such experiment came from Resource Interactive, an Ohio ad agency, who decided to take the Facebook wall to a new level with their "Off the Wall" platform. The women's retailer, The Limited, was the first company to experiment with this platform toward the end of the 2009 retail season, when it offered a product purchase of its "As Seen on Oprah" Infinity scarf direct from its wall so that consumers could make their purchase without having to leave the social networking site. The jury is still out on consumers' overall response (Resource Interactive noted that the venture had met its expectations). In its current model, Facebook receives no revenue share for the transaction.

As companies continue to struggle with positioning strategies in a flat economy, we can be certain of one thing: Facebook applications such as a the example above will continue to grow over the next several years as companies seek cost-effective strategies for connecting with consumers, and as social media tools continue to penetrate the mainstream at dramatic adoption rates.

PODCASTING POWER

Another powerful means of getting content out and forging connections that should not be overlooked is podcasting. We'll get a bit more tactical here in part, as an exercise in understanding the scope of details you must consider as you determine how to implement each of your core social media components.

An outgrowth of the Apple iPod craze in the early 2000s (hence it's name), podcasting is a technology that allows users to download their favorite music, news stories, special programs, seminars and a veritable smorgasbord of other genres through audio and/or video files from a website of their choosing.

From a desktop computer, laptop or portable music (MP3) players like the iPod or other compatible digital equipment, users can listen to or view any available content at their convenience in a time-shifted, when-it's-convenient way.

Podcast technology also allows users to create their own podcast on any topic at a modest budget and to distribute it digitally at little or no cost. This makes podcasts an attractive choice for companies looking to disseminate content in different media without having to spend precious resources.

Because of its on-demand accessibility and direct connectivity, podcasting, once relegated almost exclusively to use by individuals, is gaining increased popularity within the corporate sector as a viable information delivery system for strategic consumer marketing, along with a channel for internal and external business communications, training and education, and other useful applications.

January 2008 statistics from eMarketer.com show the total podcast audience in the United States reached more than 18 million in 2007. Projections indicate that number could nearly quadruple by 2012.

Data from eMarketer.com also project podcast advertiser and sponsorship spending could soar to $435 million by 2012, up from $165 million in 2007—so the value of this tool is decidedly real.

In fact, numbers like these are testament to a growing awareness of the medium and its expanded revenue opportunities, but more fundamentally, they suggest a paradigm shift toward sourcing more text, audio and video content from the Internet.

Advertising Age magazine sites companies with a global presence like Kraft Foods, Whirlpool, Johnson & Johnson and CIT Group, an international consulting firm, as just some of the many companies that recognize the increased utility of having integrated podcasts as an effective means of targeting specific niche markets, in ways mass media can't.

What's more, the financial implications of podcasting are undeniable—for content producers, podcasts mean little or no missed work time for traveling to present content in person, and no lodging, airfare or other related travel expenses to incur. In fact, a simple audio podcast can be done from the comfort of one's workspace with the help of some simple tools.

Costs for developing podcasts can range anywhere from a few hundred to several thousand dollars, depending on equipment (e.g., audio, video or a combination of the two) and accompanying software, set design and, at the high end of the production scale, talent.

But, before you buy any equipment, software or go out and hire some high-priced professional actors, it's important to start with some common-sense basics.

As our mantra continues throughout this book, first determine your objective. Know what you want to do, develop good, well-written topical content, then decide where you want to distribute and to whom.

Knowing your audience is a critical first step. You can gain some key insights by researching the following questions:

• What is the average age group or demographic of your audience?

• What is the typical lifestyle or psychographic profile of your audience?

• What does your audience know or not know about your product or service?

• How does your audience access information (i.e., is their primary means of accessing your brand through the web, broadcast or cable television, radio or another venue)?

• What is the preferred medium of your audience for accessing information (i.e., what is their "most-used-to-least-used" continuum)?

The answers you get may help you to better connect with your target audience and by the same token could also yield valuable information as to whether or not podcasting is a medium worth considering as a means of meeting your marketing goals. Assuming that a podcast is the right choice, the steps to planning an effective podcast are as follows:

• Select a topic of interest to your target group

• Determine a style preference (e.g., industry news, product information, consumer information, business-to-business information, a combination, etc.)

• Decide on a presentation format (e.g., audio, video or both)

• Determine whether you have and want in-house talent to deliver your message or whether you prefer and have the budget for outside professional talent

• Determine if there will be multiple people participating in the podcast presentation or whether it will be one person

• Decide on the length of the program (look at competitor podcasts or some of the top podcasts in Podcast Alley to establish a baseline)

• Decide how frequently your program will run (e.g., daily, weekly, monthly, quarterly, etc.)

• Develop and write a strong script that reflects all the information you need to include in your podcast presentation (Remember: the script is the blueprint for the final podcast production.)

Once you have considered these factors, decide on your commitment for the long term and determine a budget. You'll obviously need a means by which to record and produce your podcast, so next we turn to equipment.

Producing your podcast can be accomplished by using a PC computer that runs Windows XP or later and has at least 500-plus Megabytes (MB) of RAM, or a MAC computer that runs OS 9, OS-X or later version software with 500-plus Megabytes (MB) RAM.

On either platform, you'll also need upwards of 3 Gigabytes (GB) of hard drive space, In/Out or Microphone/Headphone jacks and a sound card or audio card (microchip circuitry that interfaces with software to facilitate the input and output of audio signals).

Another key point is to determine what presentation format your podcast will take. In other words, will the information best be delivered through an audio or through a video medium? Along these lines, too, you'll want to determine how you will distribute these podcasts (e.g., Will you make them available on your site? Submit them to Apple's iTunes? Seek widest distribution possible? Will you give them away free or will you sell them?).

When choosing between audio and video, let your product or service help you decide. If visually appealing or something that can be readily demonstrated, then a product or service video should be a top consideration. Those products or services that are driven more by information and less by visual appeal might be better suited to audio.

Regardless of your decision to go the audio or video route, you'll need a good directional microphone (e.g., one that captures sound from directly in front of you). Directional microphones are typically a good bet, compared with omnidirectional, condenser or dynamic microphones, because they are less likely to pick up extraneous ambient sound.

Macworld, recordingmagazine.com and wize.com are good resources for reviews on a variety of microphones and related equipment, but even better would be to visit your local audio store to try some out for yourself and get some advice from the pros (who typically work at those stores) as to which one will best suit your needs and your budget. Expect to spend anywhere between $150 and $1,000.

While you're at it, consider spending a few extra dollars for a device called a pop filter. This is a mesh screen that goes in front of the microphone or a foam ball that slides over the microphone to minimize those annoying "P" pops and breath noises.

Basic, easy-to-use audio editing software typically comes loaded on your PC or MAC. If you don't like the software that's included, Audacity is another free program that can be downloaded from the web and is compatible with Microsoft Windows, MAC OS-X and other operating systems.

An upgrade to multiple-track, audio-editing software products from Adobe, Sony, Steinberg and DigiDesign (makers of Pro Tools), among others, will give you that extra enhanced and more professional sound for your podcast in the $200 to $1,000 range.

Those who choose to bring several participants into their podcasts from different locations over the Internet can use a software application called Skype, which allows users to make voice calls via the web.

An accompanying call management software application, www.pamela.biz (Pamela for Skype) designed to interface with Skype, makes this an attractive tool for multiple participant podcasting.

Still, for all that Skype does, there is a definite downside, in that call voice levels often tend to be unbalanced, with one or two voices being more prominent than others on the call. One solution, noted on sitepoint.com, is for all participants to record their audio individually and then edit all segments together in post production. For those who do group podcasting routinely, this is definitely worth looking into, as you'll want to establish a consistent standard of quality from episode to episode.

One helpful tip on recording: Stereo separation (or two-channel recording) can offer you more balanced sound and better enable you to distinguish multiple voices. By the same token, a stereo format, compared with monophonic or mono format (one-channel recording), is a significantly larger file to download. That means nearly double the space on a hard drive, not to mention more production and publishing-related expense. Consider your audience and your budget before making a final decision.

Once having acquired your sound, you'll need to compress and normalize all elements before exporting your final podcast file to an MP3 format.

In short, the compression process, typically included in most software applications, levels out the loud sounds and aligns those sounds with the softer ones. Normalization boosts your compressed audio to maximize speaker capacity and gives you a full spectrum of sound.

You may come across a term in editing called bitrate. In essence, this refers to the rate at which a sampling of audio is imported. The larger the bitrate (or bit) the better the sound. Sixteen-bit audio is a typical format for an MP3 file.

It is generally a good idea to convert an audio file to a better quality 24-bit rate for editing, then convert it back to a 16-bit format for MP3 export.

If your podcast is mostly voices, bitrates in the 64 kbps to 96 kbps range will get the job done. If music is planned, you can still get a decent sound using bitrates in the 128 to 192 kbps range.

You can shoot your own podcast raw video on any of several moderately priced, good quality digital cameras and edit it using Windows Movie Maker or MAC iMovie software programs that typically come bundled and pre-installed with other software upon purchase.

Other higher-end, more professional software like Adobe Premiere, CyberLink and Final Cut Pro are just a few of many professional video software products that can give a more polished look to your final presentation. The cost here can range from $500 to $1,500.

Podcasting technology, when combined with Really Simple Syndication (RSS) technology, allows even the most technically challenged to receive, create or send whatever audio or video content is desired and post it on the Internet with relative ease.

As it relates to podcast distribution, RSS can best be described as a means through which information from multiple websites of your choosing can be consolidated into one—using aggregators (e.g., Internet companies that collect and distribute podcasts, music and product information through a single website). iTunes, Juice, iPodderX, Doppler, Podcast Ally, AOL Explorer, Internet Explorer, Libsyn, Podbean.com and Podango are just a few of many possible distribution/hosting sites. You can subscribe to as many of these sites as you choose, often at nominal fees or for free.

Once you've zeroed in on distribution, upload your MP3 file to the distribution site or create a separate host web page. Then develop a blogging system, whereby listeners who may just happen onto your podcast can share their opinions and offer often valuable suggestions. WordPress and Podcasting plug-in and Blubrry PowerPress are popular blog platforms for this.

As for the return on investment on your podcast, it can be difficult to measure in so-called hard terms. What can often be measured is the degree to which a podcast generates increased web traffic, press "buzz" and customer feedback.

Podworx.com cites podcasting as being a way to "humanize" your company through voice, and to subtly establish brand awareness and corporate image in ways a website without podcasts cannot.

On a Podworx.com podcast, Whirlpool USA is cited as using podcast technology as an effective branding tool. Through its American Family podcast, the company offers tips for simpler living, yet never mentions products or services.

Whirlpool USA is just one example of the many companies of all sizes in business, entertainment, health care, communications and virtually every other industry that have recognized podcast technology as a viable and potentially profitable information delivery system. Podcasts offer a means to drive web traffic, which drives exposure and by extension can translate into increased revenue.

Take for example, broadcast and cable mediums. If you only caught part of that all-important story or program on the radio or TV before dashing off to work or perhaps missed it altogether, go to the station or network website. Chances are, there will be a complete menu of podcasts—your story, plus a variety of others, ready to download and to be listened to at your leisure.

As for radio, a recent eMarketer report, "Internet Radio Makes Waves," notes that the shift to Internet information access has meant a double-digit dip in traditional radio ad spending in 2009 alone—$14.5 billion, which is a drop of 18% from 2008 levels.

What's more, the Radio Advertising Bureau (RAB) announced that first quarter 2009 numbers for ad spending were the industry's worst ever.

Granted, some stations are using podcasts on a regular basis. Still, radio broadcasters are in the midst of a "Radio 2020" initiative, as cited in RadioWeek, an industry trade publication, to assess and integrate new technology—like podcasting—on a broader scale as a means of reenergizing listenership.[3] In a July 2008 article

[3] National Association of Broadcasters Press Release, "Unprecedented Marketing Effort Unveiled to 'Reignite' Radio" (September 2007).
http://www.nab.org/documents/newsroom/pressRelease.asp?id=1462

cited in podcastingnews.com, UK-based global research firm Ipsos Mori indeed found that 10% of respondents who were surveyed claimed they listened less to conventional radio once starting to download podcasts.[4] Interestingly, the same study also found that 15% claimed they listened to *more* live radio since downloading podcasts, with 39% saying they tuned in to radio programs they had not previously listened to.

In a world where media convergence has become the new paradigm, it is clear that keeping pace with new and emerging technology solutions for content distribution will determine survival of the fittest.

---

[4] Ipsos Mori, "Internet Stats Compendium May 2008" (May 2008). http://www.scribd.com/doc/9372111/internetstatscompendiummay2008

13

A Blog By Any Other Name

A BLOG, SHORT FOR WEB LOG, is a website or "online journal" in which entries or posts are listed in chronological order. Blogs—in text, photo, or video form—commonly allow readers to provide comments that are posted along with the original entry. The goal of the blogger is to generate buzz within a niche. As blogs grow more and more sophisticated, they are becoming almost indistinguishable from other types of online content, and yet the value they bring is clearly unique from other types of sites.

In April 2007, David L. Sifry, founder and chairman of Technorati noted that, "Most Internet users don't even realize they are reading blogs. The distinction between blogs and mainstream media is blurring rapidly." Sites such as Huffington Post and PopEater are two such examples of blogs that go undetected as blogs, but that are well-received as Internet destinations.

SO MANY BLOGS, SO MANY BLOGGERS

According to statistics gleaned by eMarketer in May 2008, in 2007 U.S. blog readers (defined as users who read at least one blog at least once per month) totaled 94.1 million (50 percent of all adult Internet users). This number is expected to rise to 145.3 million blog readers, or 67 percent of all adult Internet users in 2012. Meanwhile, bloggers themselves (defined as Internet users who either published a new blog or updated an existing blog within a three-month period in which the research was gathered) will also continue to trend upward from 22.6 million bloggers in 2007 to what is expected to be 34.7 million bloggers in 2012.

BLOGGER BASICS

To build your blog knowledge from the ground up, we offer some blogger basics, beginning with the blogosphere, itself. The blogosphere is comprised of the community of bloggers, and when a news item captures the blogosphere's collective attention and dominates the online conversation generated by thousands of bloggers for a time (this often spills into mainstream media), this phenomenon is called a blogswarm. Most blogs include what's known as a blogroll, which is a list of blogs usually placed in the sidebar of a blog.

The blogroll is a list of recommended blogs that the blogger selects, which becomes the go-to place that aggregates content links. In this regard, the blogger can obviate the need to go anywhere else. Each blog post generates a permalink, which is a unique URL of a single blog post, as opposed to a link to the main page of the blog. This is a tremendous advantage for getting posts noticed in search.

The average blog is 500 words (the maximum word length is approximately 1,000 words), and the blog is designed to position the blogger as an expert. While the blogging statistics alone make a strong case for why your organization might consider entering the space, the real value of the blog lies in trackbacks.

Trackbacks are the system that allows bloggers to see who has written an entry on one of their original posts. The system sends a ping between blogs, which provides an alert. A reader of the original blog can read a comment about the current blog entry, which was written on someone else's blog, and the blogger commenting on the original blog entry shows to his readers a link back to the original blog entry. As podcasting innovator, Adam Curry has noted, "Links are the currency of the blogosphere."[1]

A simple blog can be created in no time using WordPress, TypePad, Google's Blogger.com, or Moveable Type, to name a few. Blogs are then captured within blog directories such as Technorati, Bloglines or Google Blog Search.

Most blogging applications are predicated on a Content Management System (CMS), which functions as the back-end application to create, edit, manage and publish digital media in the form of text, image, audio and video files. Most come with themed templates for the front-end, which are prefabricated looks and feels in which to present site content. Cascading Style Sheet (CSS)-based code controls the visual elements of a site/blog.

Most corporate brands will want to get a bit more complex that what an off-the-shelf solution can provide, but the design and programming doesn't have to be complex. The CSS coding language

---

[1] http://curry.com

used to add style (fonts, colors, spacing, layout) to blogs or web pages, separates document content from document presentation, enabling modifications to easily "cascade" throughout the entire site for theme consistency. Many companies successfully use blogware to create static websites as opposed to blogs. The beauty of this approach is that when changes to content are necessary, a non-technical user can go into the site and with little effort, update content.

Paul Gillin[2] categorizes blogs into four main types: online diaries, topical blogs, advocacy blogs and link blogs, noting that topical blogs are the most widely used and garner the biggest impact. Your resources for creating content may drive you toward one or the other, but regardless of form, keep in mind that what makes a blog so engaging is its tone and personality. Important to keep in mind is that a blog is not an institutional mouthpiece that sounds like the company is hiding behind a wall. Nor is it a marketing pitch, a one-sided conversation, a short-term commitment, or an insincere message telling people only what they want to hear.

According to research from the Fortune 500 Business Blogging Wiki, 61 (12.2%) of Fortune 500 companies are blogging (as of April 17, 2009). These entities include American Airlines, Xerox, The Clorox Company, Pitney Bowes, Chevron, Whole Foods and Johnson & Johnson. The list is as diverse as it is wide. While each of these organizations stepped into the social media space for a unique set of reasons, the strategies and pitfalls are often the same, regardless of industry type or motivation.

MyStarbucksIdea.com stands as an example of a blog that was created to collect consumer feedback on stores and products.

---

[2] Paul Gillin. *The New Influencers*, (Sanger, CA: Quill Driver Books/Word Dancer Press, Inc., June 2007).

Consumers were encouraged to submit suggestions, which were then voted on by fellow Starbucks' enthusiasts. The most popular suggestions were highlighted and reviewed by readers. The blog became so popular that it spawned a second "Ideas In Action" blog, which provides updates to users on the status of their suggested changes (e.g., introducing a new breakfast sandwich, etc.). According to Starbucks, hundreds of thousands of customer ideas have been received since its March 2008 launch leading to tangible results, such as the introduction of a "splash stick" to prevent spillage from coffee cups.

Each company will approach blogging in a different way, based in part on degrees of awareness, interest and participation across all levels of management. Whereas Sun Microsystems' CEO Jonathan Schwartz blogs as an individual, IBM has a network of employee bloggers who write about their experiences, what they're working on, or any other topic. The IBM blog highlights the people behind the products and conveys IBM's dedication to transparency and enthusiasm. Another popular corporate blog is that of Bill Marriott, based on his wonderful authenticity—enhanced by an endearing image on the site of the author in suit and tie, with his signature for an additional measure of realness.

On the political front and on the content-generation side, based on a report from BIGresearch in February 2008, U.S. registered voters ages 18 or older are blogging, with Libertarians comprising 37.6 percent of politically minded bloggers, Democrats at 26.9 percent, Independents at 25.7 percent, and Republicans at 22.9 percent.[3] This type of information is vital to anyone wishing to reach active and engaged citizens for the purposes of political support.

---

[3] BIGresearch Press Release, (February 12, 2008).
http://www.marketwire.com/press-release/Bigresearch-820299.html

Ultimately, your social media strategy should include at least a baseline understanding of where and how your target groups are engaging within the blogosphere. While a blog is undoubtedly a commitment, it is one that comes with multiple and ongoing benefits on behalf of your brand.

14

Twitter Tactics

EACH YEAR AROUND THE HOLIDAYS, we get that tingly, excited feeling, with visions of sleigh bells, eggnog and the warmth of family and friends dancing in our heads. But 2009 marked something more spectacular than any Norman Rockwell image might conjure. As Rosenbloom and Cullotta (2009) noted in *The New York Times*, 2009 hailed the first Twitter Christmas.[1]

Now, this may not seem like much to you, but it may just be a bit of a Christmas miracle. Who knew that Twitter would stick it out through confused users who didn't see the value? Who thought for a moment that this application, which as of this writing has yet to turn a profit and has instead endured the butt of every new application joke of the past two years, would blossom into what may well become the retailer's secret weapon?

And just what's prompted the uptick in usage (from 11 percent to 19 percent of all Internet users, according to Pew Internet

---

[1] Stephanie Rosenbloom and Karen Ann Culotta, "Buying Selling and Twittering All the Way," (*The New York Times*, November 27, 2009).
http://www.nytimes.com/2009/11/28/technology/28twitter.html

Research?).[2] Like any other slippery fact, this one depends on who you ask. But what we do know is that a mass-marketable value has been found that may move even the staunchest of detractors to tweet—or at least follow the tweets. Be it a discount, a secret sale, an on-site event, or a chance to win $1,000, being conveniently in the know for all things relevant to our favorite brands will push Twitter over the edge and into the mainstream.

Amidst their angst to hop aboard the social media station wagon before it leaves the driveway, retailers, in fact, have prompted a new strain of tweets that is immediately measurable and relevant. Just a smattering of tweets over a brief few weeks from brands that we follow, reveal the following uses:

Stores like Borders can tell us about an in-store discount:
30% off one item in stores and at Borders.com with this coupon >http://ow.ly/HQpi

For a holiday feel-good, Starbucks alerts us to what we can do for World AIDS Day:
Help fight AIDS in Africa spend $15 at participating US&Canada stores, get a Starbucks & (RED) CD. For each we'll give $1 to the Global Fund

In a tweet several days later, the company posts a query to the perfect pool of job applicants:
StarbucksJobs   Want to work in #socialmedia for @starbucks ? apply here: http://bit.ly/5KBZMO ^JL

---

[2] Susannah Fox, Kathryn Zickuhr, Aaron Smith, "Twitter and Status Updating, Fall 2009" (Social Networking Web 2.0, Pew Internet and American Life Project, October 21, 2009). http://www.pewinternet.org/Reports/2009/17-Twitter-and-Status-Updating-Fall-2009.aspx

From Whole Foods, we learn of budget-saving meals:

The December Whole Deal is out in stores w/ lots of ideas for a festive, budget friendly holiday season! http://bit.ly/67ZmD6 about 1 hour ago from CoTweet

And PetSmart reminds us to take our pup to the store for a pet photo with Santa:

Santa Claws is coming to your local PetSmart this weekend. Who's going? http://bit.ly/LC5uO

For pet activists, PetSmart tweets out requests such as this:

Help needed for dogs taken in Odessa puppy mill raid 12/21/09 http://bit.ly/5Kk5GR

If I'm near Odessa and I'm an animal lover, I am likely going to be eager to join in—thanks to PetSmart, who is not only a retailer, but a company that is truly concerned with helping animals.

When we added the Boston Marriott as a company to follow, we received this direct message:

Thanks for the follow! If you ever need help with hotel reservations in Boston, Cambridge or Providence, let me know - I can get you a great rate.

It's nice to know that we now "know" someone at the Boston Marriott who can get us a more exclusive deal.

Are you beginning to see what Twitter power is all about?

Ah, the mighty microblog. Microblogging is a form of blogging where users provide brief period updates (often on a frequent basis throughout the day) and publish them on micro-blogging platforms. The beauty of microblogging is that users can submit their updates via the web itself or via text messages, instant message, or even e-mail. Followers and following are the two basic actions that a user can take with another user (e.g., at last count, Lance Armstrong had a total of 2,325,474 followers, and was following 143).

The most popular microblogging tool to date is Twitter. Like Band-Aids, Kleenex and Googling (defined by Merriam-Webster as a verb meaning "to use the Google search engine to obtain information on the Internet"), Twitter has gone the way of the genericized trademark, and has come to be regarded as the very act of microblogging, itself. While there are other microblogging applications out there (e.g., Tumblr, Jaiku and Pownce—a site that closed down in December 2008), they simply have no traction when up against the pervasiveness of Twitter.

But as public relations professional Ann Wylie has noted, "Think of Twitter as a cocktail party. Spend the evening talking about what you had for lunch, and you'll soon find yourself social-izing with the chips."[3]

The Twitter website and service were created in 2006 and enable short text messages from cell phones to be sent to groups of friends and target audiences. As with most things social media, Twitter was originally an application designed for personal use to broadcast current activities and thoughts via individual text messages (mobile blogging) called "tweets," otherwise referred to

---

[3] Bill Heil and Mikolaj Piskorski, "New Twitter Research: Men Follow Men and Nobody Tweets" (Harvard Business Review, June 1, 2009)
http://blogs.hbr.org/cs/2009/06/new_twitter_research_men_follo.html

as short message service (SMS). Messages can be sent via such channels as instant messaging, Twitter's website, a user's MySpace page and a host of third-party Twitter applications.

Twitter is most powerful when used with other forms of social media because it serves as a driver to a company's core messages and thus, its core base of support. Not yet tweeting? Join the more than 80 percent of Internet users who aren't yet on board. Twitter remains massively underused—but by all accounts, this is changing rapidly. According to eMarketer, Twitter users will have grown by 200% by the close of 2009, and another 44% in 2010.

Feeling blue because you have only Mom, Dad, sis and some guy called Turtle-Z following you? No need to beat yourself up on the popularity front. The average person follows or is followed by 10 people, and the top 10 percent of Twitterers follow more than 70 people, and have more than 80 followers.[4] This means breaking through to the elite ranks of Twitter is not terribly hard at the moment—but like everything else traveling at social media warp speed, this, too, will likely change.

If you're wondering whether your target group is using Twitter, one of the best first stops is "Search.Twitter.com," which will enable you to search on a range of keywords to determine who is actively participating. This site is a launching pad for search and filter functionality that enables you to sift through real-time content and users relevant to your brand. So, for example, a search on "organic food" will yield users who are interested in this subject matter—and potential customers for your new organic foods website.

The Tweet Scan application will enable you to set up keyword searches so that you can begin "listening" to the activity within

---

[4] Ibid.

your identified market. Tweet Scan also enables users to receive e-mail alerts and back up their tweets based on a range of criteria.

The Twitter engagement is another interesting dynamic that takes place in the microblogging sphere. If you've ever signed on to follow a major brand, you may be surprised to find these companies will follow you back. You can configure your Twitter account to automatically follow those who sign on to follow you. The question you may be asking is, "But why in the world would I want to do that?" For one, you've created a unique engagement with your target group.

Let's say, for example, we decide to follow Nike. The effect of Nike, a major brand that we admire, following us back—paying attention to us as individual consumers—has an exciting dynamic attached to it. Sure, we may be cynical about Nike's ultimate motives, but for a split second we are enthralled at the connection that has been reciprocated. This can be highly effective as part of an overall brand-building strategy.

We know that the average age of status updaters is 31 (versus 27 for MySpace, 26 for Facebook, and 40-plus for LinkedIn). Twitter users tend to be more ethnically diverse and are more likely to live in an urban setting.

Twitter is an extension of other social networking. To put things into perspective, approximately 23% of social network users tweet, whereas only 4% of non-social network users do the same. In sum, use Twitter alone and you'll be tweeting alone.

The variations of Twitter applications are rampant, including such sites as StockTwits, which asks the variation of a standard tweet query, "What Are You Trading?" and has become a favorite among those who are interested in the stock market.

Some Twitter basics as you consider your corporate application: Be sure to build tweeting into your editorial calendar. Tweet when there is breaking news (e.g., Twitter was the first medium by which information was communicated out on the Mumbai terrorist attacks—prior to news outlets). Promote your brand's accompanying social networks via Twitter. Customer service is a great place to start. Companies such as Zappos, Jet Blue and Comcast lead the way in tweeting on customer service. Other uses for Twitter include generating sales leads and activities, gaining insights into customers, and growing relationships both with customers and the media.

Advice for starting: Go to Twitter.com and sign up for an account. Use your real name and avoid underscores or dots. Use a real e-mail address and create your account. Complete a profile, add a URL—to your blog, your LinkedIn site, your company's main corporate website, etc. In general for corporate brands, use the official logo. Offer useful information about what users might expect (e.g., we will post the latest product releases, discounts and secret sales). The @ symbol designates your username, so you will always want to include this in references to your Twitter account name.

Next, start connecting by finding "people" to follow. In this case, the people you follow might be your corporate competitors, like brands in your industry or organizations who are known for doing things right in this space in terms of customer service or audience engagement. You can find these companies easily by using an advanced search in Search.Twitter.com.

Like any other social networking tool, your next job is to start listening. Take a look at how competitors or role-model brands are answering the deadly question, "What Are You Doing?" Chances are, they are never actually answering that directly. Rather, it is likely they are sharing what is new or interesting, or offering a retweet (RT) of a fellow Twitterer's tweet that they think you will find useful.

Twitter has a 140-character limit—which for some is still too long (that's called Twitter humor)—so when sending tweets with long URL links, you'll want to shorten them. This is easily done using tools such as Tr.im, bit.ly, tiny.url, or owl.ly (via Hootsuite). Each URL shortening application has its own idiosyncrasies, so be sure to select the shortener that best suits your needs. Hashtags (#) are another item that breeds confusion in the Twittersphere. Hashtags are simply a way in which to index or search on a particular topic so that users can find collections of posts more easily. Hashtags are not "hardwired"—that is, they are not an official part of a Twitter account address, but simply enable users to group like tweets.

Thus, hashtags can be particularly useful for events such as conferences (e.g., #AMAConf09, #PRSA08). Hashtags can be applied to any search (e.g., #organic food, #Merry Christmas, #CA wildfires, #Oprah, #antique cars). They create immediate groups that can be useful particularly for situations in which time is a factor (e.g., tragedies, acute news updates, etc.). You can find sample hashtags when you log onto Twitter on the trending topics list.

Some other key terms are the Failwell message, which you will see at some point or another when the Twitter site is overloaded (Twitter continues to expand at a rapid rate, and thus frequent crashes have been a part of the Twitter experience). Those who sign on, tweet once and then leave are known as Twitter Quitters, which you will definitely not want your brand to become. Weight

Watchers continues to serve as the poster child for the Twitter Quitter. In February 2009, Weight Watchers launched a Twitter account, tweeted three times then left the Twittersphere. Imagine the effect this can have on a brand? Avoid this at all costs.

A Direct Message (DM) is a way to send a personal message that not everyone can see. In order to DM a Twitter user, that person must be following you (e.g., A reporter following Katie Couric could not DM her unless Couric were first following that reporter). Even if you do have a person following you whom you'd like to DM, follow the same rules that apply elsewhere: No spamming, please. And avoid pitching directly through Twitter. When a DM is appropriate and warranted, you will simply go to the right-hand side of your Twitter account page, click "DM", enter a name in the box, add your message and hit send. The nice aspect of the DM is that it does allow for additional characters, making Twitter more expandable in terms of its usefulness.

The real value of Twitter is its availability on your cell phone. Depending on the type of cell phone you have, your options for mobile Twitter client applications will vary (you can find links to applications at the very bottom of your Twitter account page, including Twitterberry for BlackBerry, etc.), but in general, in order to follow someone and receive updates via your cell phone, once you have your cell phone enabled in your Twitter account (one cell phone number per account), tweeting from your phone can be done via a short message service (SMS) aka a text message. For two-way (sending and receiving) SMS Twitter updates, simply type a text message to the standard Twitter text number (text numbers can be found at http://help.twitter.com/forums/59008/entries/14226).

For example, Twitter short codes for two-way Twitter SMS are as follows:

- US: 40404
- Canada: 21212
- UK: 86444 (Vodafone, Orange, 3 and O2 customers)
- India: 53000 (Bharti Airtel customers)
- Indonesia: 89887 (AXIS and 3 customers)
- Ireland: 51210 (O2 customers)
- New Zealand: 8987 (Vodafone and Telecom NZ customers)

So, if we wanted to follow Best Buy on our mobile phones, we would simply type the following command:

ON @BestBuy

If we were texting within the United States, we would send this message to "40404." Likewise, with any other update we post via SMS, we would send through this number.

For setting up your mobile phone, Twitter text commands and more, visit Twitter Support at: http://help.twitter.com/forums/10711/entries/14020.

You'll want to feed your own account with your company's content either via your Twitter website account, via mobile phone text message, or via Friendfeed, Tumblr, Tweetdeck, Ping.fm, or Hootsuite to name just a few Twitter clients designed to help you manage your tweets. Twitpics is great for tweeting your company's photos, while Twitvid is a good way to go for uploading video clips. Of course, you'll then want to begin promoting your company's Twitter account in other places (e.g., as a Facebook widget, on your company's blog, and using words in addition to badges such as "FOLLOW ME AT"). Promote both your hashtag and your Twitter account for optimal activity.

At all costs, you must avoid answering, "What are you doing right now?," the standard question you will find at the top of your Twitter page, which is the general culprit that has lulled many a Twitter user into offering up what he or she has consumed for lunch, along with other mundane pursuits. The better bet? Tell your readers something of value. Have a discount on a product? A special of the day? A sneak peek on a promotional sale or an interesting article pertaining to your value proposition? These value-add choices are far superior to telling us the gruesome details of your ham on rye. Ultimately, your goal with a corporate Twitter account is to influence offline activity (e.g., users going to your store for the 10% Twitter-only discount).

Some of the best reasons to tweet are to report on trends and breaking news; demonstrate a customer-centric focus; turn existing advocates into brand ambassadors; generate awareness; recruit employees to your company by posting jobs or a call for resumes; seek and create media opportunities; share best practices, ideas and information; foster customer loyalty; launch viral marketing campaigns; manage reputations; develop new contacts and pro-spective customers; promote products and services; network with existing customers; and promote contest or event participation.

When tweeting on behalf of your company, you'll need to determine if you are tweeting under your personal name on behalf of the company, or under a corporate name. This will dictate the type of tone you will want to create (e.g., Honda's tweeter is alicia@ honda). If several people are tweeting, this should be noted on the corporate bio section for full disclosure. Here again, basic rules such as ethics and proper representation of the company apply. That said, unlike other forms of communications, it would be nearly impossible to create and maintain a robust, effective Twitter presence if your corporate communications team had to step in to review every last tweet. This is why establishing guidelines and appointing the right people to the task of corporate tweeting is vital.

Once you have amassed some followers, you will want to determine who these followers are. Follow them back and see who else they happen to follow, as this can be a great way to expand your customer and potential customer base. Tweeting a couple of times per day can take five or ten minutes, so it isn't hard to manage. What can be difficult at first is striking the right balance of content based on your purpose (e.g., if you have no acute news or updates, will you post interesting links?).

Off-the-shelf design likely won't suffice for your brand. Hire a designer for a simple on-brand Twitter skin (try a Google search for "designers and Twitter", along with Craigslist or Elance.com). Beyond branding, creating your own look and feel affords you more real estate to incorporate your message (e.g., beyond the profile, messaging can be built into your Twitter design in the left- and right-hand sidebar areas). Once you are up and running and you see that someone has retweeted you, acknowledge this in your Twitter stream. Post a general thank you, or you may even want to send that follower a DM, offering to return the favor.

Twitter client applications are almost endless (e.g., Twitpoll for follower polls), but the rule of starting slow remains. As for who in your company will tweet, you may have just a designated few. But all of your C-Suite must be aware of what Twitter can do, particularly with the rise of mass tweeting direct from conferences or keynote speeches. Presenters are finding themselves caught unaware if audiences find their speeches boring, or their PowerPoint™ presentations weak at best. Word is getting out as it happens in real time, so that by the time your speech has ended, your career as a public speaker could be ruined.

Some speakers have gone so far as to position a "Twitter spotter" in the front aisle to monitor the tweets as they are sent and thus, to subtly inform the speaker of how he or she is doing, and whether it makes sense to switch topics, speed things along, move to Q&A, or simply wrap it up. For those who dislike public speaking in general, this may be one more cause to be nervous.

The key with any Twitter tactic is timely response. No response is a bad response. A slow response can sometimes be worse. If customers are taking the time to follow your brand, they expect service, attention and timeliness. Companies that have gotten it right when it comes to Twitter include H&R Block (design simplicity), Zappos (with 1,615,354 followers in December 2009), Comcast for its use of Twitter for customer support (@ComcastCares), and Whole Foods for its engaging tone and style. If your company is not prepared to put its efforts into planning and executing against expectations within the Twitter space, then hold your tweets until you are properly resourced.

Twitter is about building awareness, showing a need, having some fun and offering actionable, time-sensitive, free ways to engage. Growing a base of support is best done organically, but some smart tactics are being employed to encourage consumers to follow you.

One such success story is Moonfruit, a long-time UK technology firm, which has seen dramatic ups and downs beginning with the dot-com era. As a means of reinventing itself, Moonfruit ran a

Twitter promotion to give away 10 Apple Mac Pros—one for each year they have been in operation. The result was that it became the top trending term on Twitter three days in a row, as all people needed to do was add the hashtag #moonfruit to their tweet. An algorithm randomly chose each winner. By the second day of its promotion, Moonfruit had reached 2.5% of all Twitter traffic and the contest took the company's follower count from 400 to 47,000. More importantly, the promotion increased paying customers by 20 percent.

Or take the use of Twitter for a website like chictown.com. When users responded to owner Amy Robertson's tweets on why they liked an item, they received a coupon.

There are a range of tweeting styles or positioning strategies your company might enact: (a) The corporate brand (e.g., Four Seasons Hotel). In this case, the account is managed by a team, but the tone may be less authentic and more institutional; (b) The corporate/personal approach (e.g., Comcast accomplishes this blend with good success). On the upside, this approach can be used to build consumer trust, but it may also set false expectations of what the individual tweeters are able to do on behalf of their customers; (c) The affiliated corporate brand approach (via a personal account). In this case, the personal engagement is heightened, but the downside is the high potential to lose focus on the brand itself, along with the increased risk that the tweeter may fall off-brand); and (d) The strictly personal account with no ties to the corporation (other than perhaps a mention of employment).

The downsides to the last positioning strategy outweigh any pros, in our opinion, as the opportunities to leverage are diminished, and the relationship between individual and brand is called into question (e.g., is the individual actually authorized to speak on behalf of the brand?). That said, this can offer authenticity unlike any other option, and can yield raw consumer insights that may not otherwise be obtained.

Success in the Twittersphere is derived through knowledge and expertise, combined with a genuine interest in engaging with the community. This means being accessible. Set the expectation of when you will be tweeting (e.g., some corporate tweeters let their followers know when they will be away by posting items such as, "Have a great weekend, everyone. On Monday, we'll be sharing the results of our Twitpoll on your favorite coffee flavor."). What's the "right" number of tweets per day? In general terms, between 2 and 15 tweets per day is about right (companies with less timely information may be closer to 2 on the continuum, while companies with ongoing updates, such as media outlets or airlines will probably be closer to 15, depending on resources and tools).

If you are asked a question by a journalist or consumer, respond quickly or you'll face the added consequence of being seen as unresponsive. Again, setting clear expectations of your level of activity can go a long way.

Explore the myriad Twitter clients available (Tweetgrid, Tweetmeme, TweetDeck, Seesmic, etc.) and select one or two that may be helpful in managing your content distribution and metrics. Consider Twitter as your Public Service Announcement (PSA), where you will provide useful information (e.g., a wine tasting, book signing, tailgate party), and a link for more.

Additional tips to keep in mind: While you don't have to tweet continuously, do tweet with regularity. Be sure links work properly, and if you encounter a tweeter who has negative points to make, acknowledge the concern, but take the conversation offline. You'll want to avoid posting defensive remarks in this space because they will become a part of your company's permanent, digital record. Remember that information is always better than straight selling, and you'll want to maintain a balance—of posting new information, retweets and responses. Use compelling headlines and continue to monitor who your followers are—including what they are tweeting, who they are following, and their attitudes toward your brand. And finally, be sure that you are communicating your learnings across departments within your company. If you've received complaints on a new product, simply addressing the complaint is not enough. Inform customer service, product development and senior leadership of this feedback to take full advantage of the feedback loop.

15

Say "Community"!

PHOTOSHARING HAS BECOME a hallmark of the Internet. At its most basic, a photosharing service allows users to upload digital images from a computer, phone or directly from a camera to the Internet, in turn creating a unique address for that photo that can be retrieved from anywhere in the world. These images become part of a user's profile, which allows the user to organize and group his or her photos.

Whether it's posting pictures of Grandma's 80th birthday party for all the grandkids to see, or creating sophisticated slideshows to share on blogs and social networking sites, consumers have become accustomed to both the method and interface of photosharing services. Sites such as Flickr and Picasa have become part of many web users' regular routines.

While often eclipsed by the flashier nature of viral video, the popularity and affordability of image sharing leaves many options open for businesses. From brand building to documentation of public relations events, a smart marketer can harness the multifold opportunities presented by these services.

Photosharing can enable you to provide set images for the press or host photos for your company blog. It can also allow you to become part of a community of dedicated potential customers, as well as access a resource for marketing material on the web and in print.

Before choosing a photosharing site, it's best to have some idea of how you plan to use it to build your brand. The most basic use of these sites is as a depository for images. Most blogging software and even some web hosting companies provide little space for what could be hundreds of gigabytes worth of image data.

The photo sites can be used to host these images. For free or a small fee, photo sites can provide a place to store photos that will later be posted on your blog or website. The same is true of internal use—a photosharing site with limited access can be used within a company to share images with collaborators around the world.

The "sharing" aspect of these sites also proves useful for dealing both with traditional press and with bloggers. A restaurant, for instance, can photograph its dishes and share those high-resolution images. The images can then be included as part of a digital press packet.

Bloggers and traditional media can then use your images in their coverage. The same is true of images of public relations events. Professional photography (with permission) can be posted both on your site and as part of a sharing service. If you have a "street team," this group can post images of events to a company's page. These, too, can become part of a digital press packet, allowing press outlets to include photos of your events.

These are just the most straightforward uses, though, of photosharing services. There are more sophisticated options as well. Album creation, used to sort and organize photos, can allow a marketer to tell a promotional story using pictures. Photos can also be added to group albums, where images are collected by theme with multiple users, as a way to engage with a consumer base.

Most photosharing sites allow for "tagging" of images. Anything uploaded can be tagged. The restaurant unveiling a new pumpkin dish, therefore, can tag the image not only with the restaurant name, but also "pumpkin," "orange," "nutmeg" and so forth.

With each tag, that image becomes searchable. Users curious about pumpkin dishes, then, will see the chef's new creation. Tag clouds, popularized by Flickr, show the frequency of particular tags both on the site as a whole and within your profile.

As technology becomes more complex, sites are now also allowing "geotagging" for use with photos taken from mobile phones. The restaurant can now also geotag its images, so users who see the photographs of the new dish can now easily and simply see that the restaurant is just a few blocks away.

Geotagging, tag clouds and group sharing allow another opportunity for marketers as well. The uses already described allow a one-way conversation between the company and other users, but photosharing sites have a social aspect as well. By engaging with tags, companies can allow consumers to share images of related events by tagging the name of the business, or by sharing their own experiences with products using tags.

Geotagging also offers the unique ability to have creative promotional events where consumers can participate in scavenger hunts. Geotagged photos can also be used with other services—for instance, they can be added into Google Earth, which is a map-based system.

Use of photos, though, are governed by copyright laws. Regarding images, the collection of laws that govern the use of photos on the Internet often go through a service called "Creative Commons," which allows the creators specific legal control over the copyright of the images. "Attribution" use means that users can use and alter your images to their liking, even commercially, as long as they give you credit.

You can also use any image with an "Attribution" license under the same guidelines. Still, some consideration must be applied prior to use. In 2007, the parents of a 16-year-old child whose photo was posted under the "Attribution" license sued Virgin Mobile for use of the photo in a billboard advertisement. While the photographer had given permission for use, the girl didn't know her image was on the site. The case is still pending.

Other licenses leave more control in the hands of the creators. "Share Alike" means an image can be altered but must be released again under the same license, thus closing off most commercial ventures. "Noncommercial" allows for the image to be used and altered, as long as it's not for commercial purposes. Finally, we have "No Derivative works," which means the work must be shared verbatim. All require proper attribution to the creator.

Many choices exist for marketers looking to start photosharing, each with its own advantages. Many sites are also owned by larger companies, and their interfaces mesh with those of their parent corporations, allowing the savvy marketer to create a holistic digital interface. Below are just some of the more popular choices in photosharing:

Photobucket: Owned by Newscorp, Photobucket hosts not only pictures but also video. Aside from regular albums, you can create scrapbooks and slideshows. The Pro version also allows FTP upload and increased storage.

Flickr: One of the most social sites, Flickr is owned by Yahoo! Inc. and allows cross-platform relationships. Flickr is also considered the creator of the "tag cloud" concept and allows limited video uploads.

Picasa: The Google-owned, image-sharing service integrates well with Google's other offerings and provides many built-in editing features such as cropping and red-eye reduction.

Shutterfly: This service hosts unlimited photos at unlimited resolutions, making it particularly good for hi-resolution images.

Snapfish: Also allows for unlimited storage, but encourages the purchase of associated "products," such as mugs and calendars.

Facebook: While Facebook has fewer photo features than some of the other sites, it innovated "tagging" and incorporates well with social-networking-based marketing strategies.

Regardless of which photosharing application(s) you choose, your brand's pictures really are worth a thousand words, so incorporating images into your strategy is smart positioning.

16

I Want My YouTube

S ANYTHING MORE COMPELLING than video? And we don't mean the content. From content aggregation, to search, to its potential to drive return, video is not only the new wave; in many ways it's the only wave for accomplishing multiple tasks in just one space.

Video sharing allows users to upload and share videos to video sharing websites such as YouTube. Users can watch the videos, comment on them, share them with other users and even embed them within their own websites and blogs. More and more companies are creating video content to share on video-sharing websites like YouTube to promote their brands and offerings. Often this is done through the creation of a vlog. Cousin to the blog, the vlog differs only in so much as it showcases video. While YouTube is the Goliath, other video aggregators and distributors do exist, such as Vimeo, Viddler, blip.tv and Hulu.

Internet users view online video, and with the proliferation of technologically advanced mobile devices, that number grows each day. Savvy companies can harness the power of online video to achieve a number of marketing goals, including branding, product placement and increased sales.

But making Internet video marketing work requires more than just capturing content and uploading it to YouTube. It requires thought, planning, hard work and a lot of creativity to sort through the many options and approaches available to marketers to make their content stand out and their digital campaigns effective.

Online video is one of the most flexible marketing media imaginable and can allow for amazing consumer engagement. For the most part, the web videos consumers watch are ones they are dedicated to seeing—unlike passively watching television, they are actively connecting with the video, not muting your message or taking a bathroom break. As a result, web video has to be ready to engage consumers on the same high-engagement level and must offer them something unique, interesting, entertaining and valuable in order for this content to be worth your company's investment.

Like any social networking scenario, there are many different approaches to hosting and distributing web video. The first question to ask yourself is how you want to present your video. That is, how will you "host" your content? Most effective web video is displayed using a software plug-in called Adobe Flash, and in order to take the raw form of your video—the file exported from your video-editing software—the video must be translated into that language. How to host the video, or make it Flash-readable for the greatest number of web viewers, requires finding some method or service. There are two primary choices: your own dedicated channel presented on your company's website or blog, or on one of the many social-network-style web hosting services. Cost, control and shareability are all concerns when selecting such a service.

To completely control the presentation of your web video, there are a number of services that allow you to display your video only how you'd like it, whether that means a single video or creating a "channel" of related videos for consumers. The first and most expensive requires your servers to host the videos and a pro-grammer on staff to manage posting the videos to your website. It requires using a great deal of bandwidth and posting and creating video becomes more complex, but you have absolute control over display and use.

There are other services, paid and otherwise, that will offer that same level of control for little or no cost. Called online video platforms, they host the file of the video for use on the web. Brightcove is the corporate favorite for this type of display and manages the videos for companies like Discovery.com and The New York Times. Marcellus, another online video platform, works much the same way and hosts videos for companies like the BBC. These services are completely customizable and integrate with your content management system, but are expensive.

Viddler offers a similar service, but includes a free option (with third-party advertising) or the option of becoming an advertising partner (for a fee). The video player itself can be tailored to fit the look and feel of your company's website or blog and can display your logo. Viddler, unlike Marcellus or Brightcove, offers timed commenting, where audience members can comment on specific parts of a video.

For considerably less money, more shareability and greater ease of use, companies can choose social-media video platforms.

Videos are posted to your site and usually to the sharing site as well. The services take care of encoding the video into Flash and hosting the file, but because your company is dependent on the bandwidth and service, you have less control over the videos themselves. One such service is Vimeo. Using Vimeo commercially is difficult. The site offers hosting and high-quality display using high bit rates and high definition, and has a dedicated, supportive community, but it does not allow directly commercial video use for companies without developing an advertising partnership.

That said, there are some groups exempt from this ban. Non-profits and religious organizations may use Vimeo as they please. Furthermore, musicians, authors, filmmakers and other artists can use Vimeo as a promotional tool. Videos can be embedded into websites, but only with the Vimeo player, and the site itself is centered on the idea of social networking and as a result, has a tight-knit community of viewers.

Similarly, Blip.tv will host video free (with advertising) or for a nominal fee (no advertising), but is designed for episode-style video, commercial or otherwise. If your company has opted to create reoccurring content, like a show centered around product placement, or a series of neighborhood or home tours, a service like Blip will help you create your own channel and market it both within the Blip community and on the web.

Facebook and MySpace also offer hosting. Sharing these videos outside of the Facebook and Myspace communities is difficult and the quality of video is low, but if your social networking campaign and video campaign are closely tied, then they may be good options. Other sites, like Hulu.com or FunnyorDie.com host video, but generally of a more specific and less user-generated variety.

The three biggest players in the market for general sharing are Metacafe, Dailymotion and YouTube. All three allow uploads and various fee and partnership opportunities, along with embedding within your company's website or blog. Of the three, YouTube is the most popular and well-known. As with other major Internet players like Facebook, some presence on YouTube is expected, and even if you host your video with another service, cross-posting is a viable option. Virtually all video-capable mobile phones support YouTube.

Created in 2005, YouTube is the second largest search engine next to Google, though many are only now beginning to realize the dreaminess of YouTube as a mechanism for search. Some statistics to give you context: YouTube has an average of more than 60 million unique visitors, and on average, 10 hours of video footage is uploaded to the site every minute—*every minute.*

The site hosts over 100 million videos every day, and has billions of hits each month. Owned by Google, it accounts for nearly 25% of that site's searches—making it the second biggest search engine in the world. That means two things for marketers. When people are looking for online video, they turn to YouTube, but there's also an unwieldy amount of video on YouTube for consumers to look at—so making your content stand out is paramount.

In the past, your company may have contacted its public relations firm to gather costs on making a video to promote an upcoming product launch. The public relations firm would put its best people on the job to come up with a news angle that might garner some pick-up on the 11 o'clock news.

Today, any company can essentially create its own network or channel for video distribution—with as much product hype or news value as it likes. Production costs can be relatively low, and cost for distribution is virtually free—at least, for now.

That's when content becomes so significant. Technically, the phrase "viral video" means any site passed around from friend to friend—"this is interesting," or "take a look at that." But in the eyes of many marketers, viral video has become the Holy Grail— making the perfect random video that takes the Internet by storm and builds your brand in the process. But Internet audiences are fickle. Thus, as marketers set out to create video that is cheap, quick and entertaining while building the brand and maintaining authenticity for what may be minimal returns, the exercise should be less about going "viral" and more about smart branding.

Some approaches, like Burger King's Chicken Man on the street or Starbucks' "Love is All You Need" campaign are effective because they are entertaining and aimed at their respective audiences. Because viewers can choose what they're watching on their own, it is necessary for that content to be something appealing, though, and if it seems disingenuous, it won't achieve the "You've got to see this" status required for a high ROI.

But the wacky approach isn't always necessary. One of the biggest video categories on the Internet is "how-to" clips. From how-to videos to answering frequently asked questions, consumers use Internet video for things other than laughs. Integrating your brand with that type of video, like Singer's sewing machine tutorials or Kraft Foods' cooking channel will strengthen your brand, provide a service to your customers, and be more directly involved with your overall goals than trying to come up with a funny or random video spot. Similarly, interviews with people in your company, like a chef discussing her education or your executive talking about the company's philosophy, can be inexpensive, honest and direct ways to engage with customers.

World leaders have utilized video effectively to shape their personal brands—from President Obama's taped weekly addresses on his own channel (BarackTV), to the Queen of England visiting the poor, or Queen Rania of Jordan, who won the YouTube Visionary Award for her goal of helping to prevent cultural stereotyping as told via video.

On the corporate side, the case of Blendtec is the legendary example of what video can do for a company and its product. As CEO Tom Dickson was busy blending all manner of items in usual fashion to test the ruggedness of his blenders, a colleague happened by and offered to videotape the event. He then offered to upload the video onto YouTube, and the rest is history—and more importantly, profit.

The videos caught on, and became a low-cost, instant viral hit (e.g., they produced eight episodes, which yielded 3 million downloads in just one week). The most famous "blend" was that of the iPhone, and the company continues to take requests. (You can watch the video from Blendtec's YouTube channel at http://www.youtube.com/blendtec.) Dickson reported a "five-fold increase in sales"—not too shabby for otherwise humble product testing.

Hotel owners and restauranteurs can show tours of their locations, salons can record a styling session or other services and real estate agents can provide images of their listed properties. These types of videos don't get thousands of views, but the views they do get are more valuable because they are providing context for an interested consumer. Viral-style videos are the equivalent of yelling in a crowded mall, while these more direct shots, while still interesting and entertaining, are like an intimate discussion with a friend.

Furthermore, web video can be as expensive as you want to make it. Setting aside hosting costs, creating a video can be as cheap as opening up a computer and talking into a webcam, or as expensive as a television commercial. To make testimonial-style video, all you need is a camera on a steady surface and someone who knows the basics of video editing in one of the nominally priced or free packages that come with most computers. For more advanced video, it's up to your budget constraints.

Slick videos with high production value can be expensive, but a person on staff with editing skills, a good camera and quality software like Final Cut Pro can cover most of your basic needs. Choosing which option depends on what your goals are, how competent your staff is, and how you plan to use the video.

17

Widget Mania

"<HEART> WIDGETS." This is the slogan on the T-shirt we keep meaning to have screen-printed as a tribute to these handy tools for bringing content to consumers.

In old textbooks about marketing and economics, a "widget" was an imaginary product (usually manufactured by the equally imaginary "Acme Corporation") used to illustrate basic business concepts.

Today, widgets are very real, even though they reside on computer desktops, Facebook pages and mobile phones. These free, fun, functional applications provide real-time news and weather reports, act as clocks, stock tickers and calculators, and sometimes simply entertain bored commuters and cubicle dwellers.

Simply stated, web widgets (aka, badges, gadgets or mini-applications) are tiny, interactive micro-applications comprised of small portions of code that can be easily embedded into a blog site (e.g., YouTube), or run in a widget platform installed on the user's own computer.

This code or program brings in "live" content, such as news, ads, links, images or videos—from a third-party site without the website owner having to update it.

These widgets are often displayed on users' profile pages on Facebook and other social networks, and then sent in e-mail messages within these networks to their friends.

Widgets have been around for about a decade, but they really took off in 2004, when the original Mac-only Konfabulator mini-apps were finally made available to Windows users. This cross-platform compatibility sent widget development and popularity into the stratosphere. Widgets were an easy way to receive automatic information updates, delivered in an appealing, light-weight "package" that was non-intrusive but ever present.

Clever marketers soon realized that widgets were the ultimate "opt-in"—a cheap, easy (and, hopefully, viral) way to keep consumers connected to their brand.

One key ingredient to widgets is Real Simple Syndication (RSS). We have mentioned RSS elsewhere as a syndication format that allows websites and blogs to distribute their updated, dynamic content as feeds to users. Instead of having to visit the website, users can sign up for the feed provided by the website or blog and using an RSS reader or aggregator (e.g., Google Reader, Bloglines, Feedburner), access the feed. In general terms when it comes to RSS, users can sign up for as many feeds from different websites as desired and then access and manage those feeds all at once using their RSS reader. In widget terms, if you can pool feeds into your branded widget application, your application will become that much more valuable to consumers who are hungry for time-shifted, packaged, convenient helpings of content.

In a widely reprinted piece in Advertising Age, Bob Garfield famously called widgets "Websites-in-a-Can."

"Branded widgets are the refrigerator magnets of the Brave New World," he wrote. "They carry an ad message wherever they go":

> *"That's at a minimum. At a maximum, the widget is something like the magical connection between marketers and consumers, not only replacing the one-way messaging long dominated by media advertising but vastly outperforming it. Because online the link is literal and direct, and along its path, data of behavior, preference and intention are left at every step. Oh, and your target consumers actually go out searching for your branded gimcrack. Oh, and they display it within easy reach. Oh, and they pass copies along to their friends and associates. Oh, and because they've been turned on by a friend, they are hospitable and receptive recipients. And, oh, in case this didn't quite register the first time I mentioned it, the barriers to entry are preposterously low."[1]*

So what's the catch? Ironically, all the things that make widgets so appealing contain the seeds of their potential drawbacks.

Do-it-yourself sites like WidgetBox.com make it easy for anyone to build a widget. And probably not everyone should, anymore than "anyone" can or should design a corporate website or write direct mail copy.

This means that widgets are everywhere now. Each one is striving to be seen in world of media overload, in which consumers

---

[1] Bob Garfield, "Widgets Are Made for Marketing, So Why Aren't More Advertisers Using Them?" (*Advertising Age*, December 2008).

are fickle and easily bored. Because they're free and often frivolous, widgets are often the first things dragged to the trash when users unclutter their desktops.

A few savvy companies have created popular widgets with lasting appeal. They all emphasize functionality, visual appeal and ingenuity. For example:

• Nike's "Miles" 3D desktop widget tracks a runner's progress, offers timely local weather reports and lets users know about upcoming running events—and Nike promotions, of course.

• Those who choose the UPS widget can schedule and track shipments in a couple of clicks.

• Backcountry.com's widget alerts shoppers to special deals.

• "Hosted" by an attractive young woman, Johnnie Walker's "Jennie" widget tells travelers where to find the nearest "cool" local watering holes.

• The Centers for Disease Control's H1N1 widget packs news, facts and tips into a deceptively compact "package." At the same time, a Food and Drug Administration widget details the truth about "fraudulent H1N1 products," from "antiseptics" to "teas."

• A "Quidditch Trainer" widget promoting "Harry Potter and the Half-Blood Prince: The Videogame" lets young wizards in training earn rewards and "get magical downloads."

- Fidelity Market Monitor is a completely customizable stock tracker that also monitors market news and conditions.

As always with all things related to social media, ROI measurement is an inexact science. Jodi McDermott of Clearspring advises marketers to ask themselves:

"How many times was the widget grabbed successfully? How many times was the widget shared successfully? How fast is the widget spreading? Does the number of widget installs double every n days? How does that compare to other widgets that you have released into the wild? Keeping track of the 'Days to double' is an interesting metric that will trend down over time—but is a good yardstick in comparing the speed of widget distribution."[2]

In 2008, Sony subtly rebranded its existing "Vampires" Facebook widget to promote the horror movie *30 Days of Night*, including a sweepstakes to try to increase interest. Sony received close to 60,000 sweepstakes entries, with 10,000 entries having been originally pegged as the metric for success.

Silicon Valley strategist Jeremiah Owyang attributes the widget's success to understated, well-integrated branding; real value in the form of a generous sweepstakes; and a perfect match between widget and audience.[3]

---

[2] Jodi McDermott, "Measuring The Virality Of Widgets" (Online Metrics Insider Magazine, August 2008). http://www.mediapost.com/publications/?fa=Articles.showArticle&art_aid=89036
[3] Jeremiah Owyang "Case Study: How Sony Leveraged A Popular Vampire Facebook Widget To Reach Its Community"(January 2008). http://www.web-strategist.com/blog/2008/01/29/case-study-how-sony-leveraged-a-popular-vampire-facebook-widget-to-reach-its-community/

Best practices regarding widget marketing emphasize common sense and a user-oriented focus:

• Answer the question: Why would someone want to download this? What problem does it solve? How does it make someone's life easier?

• Keep it simple: Don't ask downloaders for e-mail addresses or other personal information. Users are far more likely to download a widget that's completely free, no strings attached.

• Make it easy for users to share the widget with friends. If possible, build in a "sharing menu" allowing users to share it via platforms like Gigya and Clearspring. (These platforms also let you track your widget's popularity and other aspects of activity.)

• Let users customize and personalize the widget.

• Make sure your widget is compatible with multiple platforms. Test and test again. This may mean your widget must be designed in multiple versions (e.g., Google, Yahoo, iPhone).

• Keep widgets small, both in terms of physical size (think of the size of a credit card) and memory.

• Get listed in widget directories and "galleries" like Widgetbox and iGoogle.

- Widgets can support audio and video, but don't use "autoplay" as the default setting. Let users decide when to listen and watch.

"Widgets should be part of a long-term strategy," explains Kailee Brown of Ignite Social Media:

> *"It's not reasonable to develop a widget for the purpose of a two-week campaign. Also, it's necessary to consider what happens with the widget once you're done with the campaign. You should never abandon a widget. There is nothing worse than finding a widget you want to use and realizing it doesn't work. That doesn't support brand favorability. If you develop a widget correctly, it will always be available and useful. And trust me, you will then benefit from the long-tail installs of the widget."[4]*

As Clearspring advises widget developers: "Make it an app, not an ad." Remember: You care more about your brand than potential downloaders do. Every widget should be functional first and a branding device second.

Everybody hopes for their widget to "go viral," but most authors who dream of being on Oprah don't get their wish, either. "Viral" can't be faked or bought. Be realistic.

As cell phone and smart phone sales explode, the future of the widget is a global, mobile one. One 2009 report on future trends forecasts increasingly quick adoption of mobile widgets. The

---

[4] Kailee Brown, "8 Questions to Ask When Developing Widgets for Social Media Marketing" (Ignite Social Media Agency, April 2009). http://www.ignitesocialmedia.com/8-questions-to-ask-when-developing-widgets-for-social-media-marketing/

enormous popularity of iPhone apps and their many imitators shows no sign of receding in the near future, so marketers need to be out in front.[5]

Search giant Google is seen as "a key distribution channel for mobile widgets" and is looking to "web app development as the future of successful mobile platforms."

As with all evolving technological trends, the future of widgets in terms of social media and marketing is in constant flux. To this end, may we recommend a widget designed to keep marketers up to date on widgets? Now there's a popular download!

---

[5] From Research and Markets, "Mobile Widgets Market: Current and Future Trends, Key Drivers, Players, Issues and Recommendations" (August 2009). http://www.researchandmarkets.com/research/6b3782/mobile_widgets_mar

18

Brandstreaming:
Managing Inputs and Outputs

OR THOSE WHO ARE JUST ENTERING the social media space, lifestreaming may be the last thing you are ready to consider—but it might be your best first move. Wordspy defines lifestreaming as "an online record of a person's daily activities [both online and offline], either via direct video feed or via aggregating the person's online content such as blog posts, social network updates, and online photos."

Experts such as Steve Rubel of Edelman have migrated to this means of content generation as a more effective means of creating a pervasive and unified online presence that is also manageable. Applications such as FriendFeed and Posterous enable this.

Blogger Michael Fruchter offered this overview of lifestreaming in September 2008:

I was thinking about all the data we lifestream. What does this data say about us? How valuable is this data in the right corporation's hands? Bookmarks are very telling of an individual's mindset, habits and interests. The same interpretations can be made about the data we lifestream. A person's digital fingerprint is a potential goldmine of data for various industries.[1]

From a marketing perspective, tracking consumer behavior will take on a whole new meaning when captured through consumers' lifestreams. Hence, from the corporate marketing perch, we arrive at yet another adaptation of a tool designed to stream the average person's day as a personal, dynamic account, to become a means of showcasing brands in a concentrated and impact-driven way. Brands such as Nissan, Dairy Queen, Microsoft and Ford are just some examples of companies who have put brandstreaming to work.

Some of the low-hanging fruit in brandstreaming takes the form of creating a consistent online brand identity and aggregating content in a centralized place to better tell your brand's story and to foster audience interaction with your content.

From a content management standpoint, companies who enter the social media space realize quickly the need to streamline and disseminate messages across multiple social networking sites. Depending upon the type of corporation and its messages, determining which lifestreaming platform to use will vary based on the need to update remotely from a mobile device versus direct from e-mail, desktop or the web.

There is no exact science to a company's brandstream. Like any other aspect of marketing, the mix will depend upon the nature of

---

[1] Mike Fruchter on Social Media, "What does your digital fingerprint say about you?" (September 2008).
http://www.michaelfruchter.com/blog/2008/09/what-does-your-digital-fingerprint-say-about-you/

the brand and its ultimate objectives. Some elements to consider may be corporate news and information about the organization, content from executive leadership on the state of the industry, trends or outlooks, or even the corporate culture, itself, where a company might produce a "day-in-the-life" stream of content.

Brandstreaming is centered on the idea of curating content from a range of media and presenting it in a platform that is seamless and easy to access for consumers. Why is this becoming so important? We are seeing a trend on the rise in which content is no longer being accessed direct from its published location. Rather, it is being accessed through aggregation via RSS feeds, personalized start pages, social networking sites, widgets, readers and platforms designed specifically to pool and curate information.

Statistics place consumer demand for personalized start pages at approximately 60 percent and growing.[2] With the flood of social networking applications, information sources and content sites available, managing this daily flow can become unmanageable in no time. Consumers' appetites for quality content have not diminished, but they now want their content served up in one all-you-can-consume buffet delivered to their doorsteps.

On the corporate side, marketers are excited by the possibilities of lifestreaming and brandstreaming because of the rich consumer behavior data they will be able to collect and analyze. Brandstreaming allows for the melding of traditional blogs, social networks, photo and videosharing sites, microblogs and more into a conglomerated presence of shareable, interactive content.

Some of the more popular platforms for brandstreaming include Posterous, which enables users to upload any form of

---

[2] Razorfish, "Consumer Experience Report" (2008).
http://www.slideshare.net/andre4e/razorfish-consumer-experience-report-2008-presentation

content from video, to photos, to tweets and more. The beauty of this application is that it can all be accomplished through e-mail.

Friendfeed is another such platform that enables users to create, publish and share content via a multitude of channels. In similar fashion, Tumblr enables posting of multimedia to a broad range of sites from a mobile device, desktop or e-mail. Then there is Lifestrea.ms, whose description reads:

> *Think of LifeStrea.ms as of a brand new, web based e-mail client, which brings you all kinds of messages from a broad selection of social networks:*
>
> *You get all your friends' status updates from Twitter, their messages from Facebook and their latest photo uploads from MySpace—all in one place.*[3]

This platform enables the user to comment on, receive comments on, post, reply, forward and update to a multitude of social networking sites, saving users from having to access five different sites to send the same update.

The list of lifestreaming and brandstreaming sites is almost endless, but the takeaway is finite: The magnitude of sites to which consumers have, want or need access is unsustainable. Lifestreaming is as much about necessity as it is about convenience, and the smart marketers are infiltrating these applications now— even as many consumers are still trying to distinguish between a follower and a fan.

Like everything else, your brandstream will ebb and flow based on consumer response. You may find yourself eliminating streams

---

[3] http://lifestrea.ms/

that are creating more clutter than content, and adding connections that are picking up traction. Here again, don't expect that if you build a brandstream they will come.

If you decide to use a third-party vendor, you'll need to promote this site on other sites and locations—and not just on your marketing campaigns, but in your social media and traditional press releases, in your company newsletter, on your brand's main website, and in direct-to-consumer communications.

Keep in mind that because brandstreaming is the equivalent of real-time blogging, your commitment to updates and ongoing content will likely increase, even as brandstreaming enables you to streamline the process.

PART III

Bring It

M ost companies understand that they need to create a social media presence, and they understand they must show tangible results. This often leads to the running leap at mass acquisition of fans and followers at the expense of really stopping to understand how a company's engagement in social media will forever change not only how customers see the brand, but how the company sees the brand as well. This is a direct result of thoughtful planning, careful implementation, and knowing when to press "Go"—in essence, knowing when and how to "bring it" in a convergence that allows your brand to dominate within its industry. This includes understanding how you will measure success before you venture out.

19

Web 2.0 Resource Procurement:
Your Social Media Team

COMPANIES TODAY ARE FACED not with the question of *if* when it comes to including social media; they are faced with the questions of "when" and "how." Based on our work with clients across industries, we have found that many struggle with the parameters of what it takes to launch a social media campaign the right way. For example, they ask questions such as "How many dedicated staff will this effort require?" and "How many existing staff will we need to recruit, and what might be the time commitment?"

While these answers will vary depending on the nuances of your organization, once your company has established a policy and a plan, it is time to set up your team of employees to establish, monitor and develop the company's online presence.

The keyword is "team." It is unwise to simply dump "that social media stuff" onto a single employee, no matter how enthusiastic or "tech savvy" that person may be. No single person possesses the expertise in public relations and marketing and customer service to competently engage with everyone he or she will "meet" on the web.

And remember: one day that employee might not be your employee anymore. When employees charged with social media leave, their intimate knowledge of the company's online "universe," with all its non-transferable nuances, goes out the door with them, along with that cardboard box full of photos and mugs. Like any other smart corporate marketing initiative, you'll want to have some depth on the bench.

IMPORTANT NOTE: Oftentimes because accounts are set up by an individual user, with his or her individual (and sometimes personal) e-mail account, companies can find themselves "locked out" unexpectedly from their own social media sites. This can happen innocently enough (e.g., if a company must establish multiple social networking accounts, this often entails the need for multiple e-mail addresses). Rather than creating accounts with an individual's e-mail address, your smarter first move is to create multiple corporate e-mail addresses and passwords for the purposes of your social media team. All accounts should be stored in a secure or password-protected space, but should be accessible and known to those who will need them.

Like any other proprietary access, staff shouldn't be taking their access to the company's social media accounts with them when they go. Work with your IT group to develop a bulletproof method to keep former staffers from accessing, and possibly sabotaging these platforms. From the very beginning, set up and brand all social media accounts using company e-mail addresses, rather than employee@gmail.com. In addition, all employment contracts should specify that the company owns access to, and the content of, these social media accounts, not the employee; require HR to stay current on evolving legal standards in this regard.

Teamwork is also essential because insights gleaned from all those social media efforts are useless if they don't filter down (or up) to others in the organization. Customer service needs to know about persistent complaints via Twitter, for example, while PR has to read that influential blogger's scathing post.

Individual departments are more likely to take action if they are participating directly in social media, not just receiving yet another weekly report they're too busy to read.

To this end, you'll want to ensure that your social media "team" really is a team—in practice and not just on the "white board" organizational chart, advises Chris Brogan, President of New Marketing Labs. He's observed that:

"Sometimes a company will have a few more employees [involved in social media efforts], but then they're just shadows of the functions of the main person doing it. A team isn't made up of only quarterbacks.

"We're building a cluster of solo players out there on the field when what is necessary is a team methodology with all kinds of touch points, system connectors, and deeper communications/ strategy channels."[1]

The growing consensus among social media experts like Brogan is that the optimal staffing scenario involves assembling a team of existing employees, across various departments.

Start out with as large a group as possible; it will be easier to winnow out team members later than to add them after the fact.

---

[1] Chris Brogan, "Social Media Needs To Become a Team Sport" (November 2009). http://www.chrisbrogan.com/social-media-needs-to-become-a-team-sport/

Select a regular meeting schedule, perhaps weekly, for collaboration. Such meetings will look forward as well as backward: instead of just reciting the number of hits the blog received in the last seven days, request briefings on upcoming events, promotions or product launches, then brainstorm how best to leverage social media to promote them.

Vital to ensuring follow-through is the establishment of a social media editorial calendar. As a baseline, this will include standard content updates (e.g., weekly blog, minimum number of daily tweets, update schedule for Facebook, which staff will be assigned to these items, etc.). Unless you are prepared to mainstream these deliverables as you would any other element of marketing, communications, or public relations, your efforts will remain sporadic, sidebar initiatives.

Referring back to the social media policy, continue to clarify which team members are empowered to participate online as well as how, along with new challenges as they present themselves.

In a large company, says Amber Naslund, author of Building a Social Media Team, team members would represent corporate communications, public relations, marketing, brand/product management, customer/client service, business development and sales, human resources, IT and legal and/or investor relations.

"For a smaller company without large, independent departments," adds Naslund, "you can probably have one or two people act as your information gatherers through your listening tools, and report back to the rest of the team on a regular basis about what's happening."[2]

---

[2] Amber Naslund, "The Social Media Team Toolkit: Listening" (April 2009). http://altitudebranding.com/2009/04/the-social-media-team-toolkit-listening/

(She adds that too many companies get bogged down at the very start of the process by wondering where social media falls in their organizational chart. Naslund points out that such questions matter more to the company than they do to its customers, who just want to be treated professionally by whoever reads their tweets or blog comments.)

Having a team also means you can do more than just monitor mentions of your brand, put out customer service "fires" and scan the company blog for negative comments. For large corporations, team involvement in social media inspires and facilitates special promotions and fan-base building exercises that a single employee could never accommodate.

For example, Harley-Davidson's Facebook fan page features 9,000 photos of owners with their bikes, while Six Flag's more than doubled its number of Facebook fans after asking enthusiasts to vote for their favorite roller coasters. Customers can suggest and vote on ideas at the Starbucks site, some of which have since been adopted by the company. Dell maintains a variety of online platforms; they even have their own "company island" in the Second Life virtual world.

That's another reason experts like Naslund and Brogan also generally advise companies against outsourcing social media tasks if possible. A part-timer, consultant or "ghost tweeter" who isn't embedded in the company is less likely to "get" the corporate culture and thus represent it authentically online.

Teamwork is the ideal, but realistically, hiring or training one person to handle social media may be the only option some enterprises have right now. Increasingly, newly minted "community animators," also known as "community managers," are the ones taking on the responsibility of corporate social media for a single firm.

"The community manager is the brand steward within the community of customers, prospects and partners that you serve," explains Dana VanDen Heuvel. "They are advocates, ambassadors and stewards of the brand in one."[3]

Tactful and talented, community managers are tasked with listening and communicating in all online channels, not just with customers, but with others in the same industry. They set up key-word-specific online tracking alerts, keep up with the latest trends and technical developments, and read and comment on blogs.

The perfect candidate for the job of community manager is someone who is always ready to ask, "How can my company be useful, relevant and helpful to the community we serve?" says VanDen Heuvel, "A sharing, caring and 'ready to educate' mentality is a must, as are technical, interpersonal and project/team management skills."[4]

Brogan suggests measuring this community manager's performance based upon the following benchmarks:

• They respond to blog comments and other messages in less than 24 hours

• They leave meaningful comments on appropriate industry-related blogs, video sites and other appropriate online "gathering places"

---

[3] Dana VanDen Heuvel "Hiring for Social Media Positions" (Inspire Blog, September 2009). http://www.smartmarketers.com/2009/09/hiring_for_social_media_positi.html
[4] Ibid.

• They've grown the number of subscribers/comments/links to the company's online properties

• They post quality information on the organization's blog, and link to other interesting posts elsewhere on the web

• Their efforts increase the links from other sites to the company's blog/site

• Their efforts have helped increase attendance at company events, subscriptions to its newsletter and other measurables

Kipp Bodnar, Social Marketing Manager and contributor to *Digital Capitalism*, believes any candidate for the position of community manager must be able to answer "yes" to the following questions:

• Have they helped companies use social media in the past?

• Do they actively participate themselves? (On blogs, podcasts, Twitter, etc.)

• Did they answer "What is the first thing you would do in leading social media at [company X]?" with a statement referring to research and monitoring?

• How do they consume information? (They should include RSS, blogs, podcasts, FeedReader, aggregation, and Twitter search in their response.)

- Have they worked for or with agencies on social media campaigns?[5]

Bodnar warns: "If the person you are interviewing says they are an expert at all aspects of social media, then that is the end of the road for them, they are clearly a pretender and not a contender."[6]

Self-proclaimed "social media experts" are cropping up at a predictably rapid rate. Recognized credentials don't exist—there's no such thing as a Bachelors of Social Media (yet). Ironically, in such a brave, new, unchartered world, wisdom suggests a reliance upon old-fashioned "human resources" standards: great references, a blend of technical know-how and interpersonal skills, plus an impressive portfolio. As Kipp Bodnar puts it: "Social Media is new, but hiring isn't."

---

[5] Kipp Bodnar, "Uncase Study: How Aflac Should Assemble a Social Media Team to Build for Long-Term Success" (Digital Capitalism Blob, February 2009).
[6] Ibid.

20

It's the Metrics, Stupid

F YOU MAKE THE INVESTMENT of time and money to launch efforts in this space, establish your system for tracking first. There are a number of handy programs for tracking activity—some single-application-based, some that capture multiple applications and lifestreaming, in which a user's full scope of social media activity can be captured and tracked in one stream.

But not all applications—free or purchased—can do all things (e.g., some will track multiple Twitter accounts, but won't track Facebook, etc.), so chances are high that you may require more than one tool for measurement in order to measure each important aspect of your potential return.

The more money and effort you allocate for social media, the more your bosses are going to want to see returns. In any economy, no one wants to throw valuable resources (including your time) down a hole. That's why it's important to have a strategy from the very beginning for measuring the effectiveness of your efforts.

We continue to hear from companies who say, "Well, we'll just get up and running first, and then we'll start thinking about tracking." But the time to get at the metrics—and those of your competitors—is truly at the onset.

In the midst of the rush to jump on the social media bandwagon, create a presence, produce content and aggregate consumers based on focused interests, marketers and communicators must keep at the forefront one of the most attractive elements within this space: Everything is measurable.

Some of the standard metrics you will want to consider, based on your objectives are:

• Time On Site (TOS)
• Number of mentions on blogs
• Number of positive/negative ratings on products
• Number of comments on content
• Number of pieces of user-generated content uploaded (e.g., video)
• Click-throughs to site
• Return On Investment (time, money)

In order to tap into the richness that this environment provides, you must have some idea of what you're looking to gain from your social media expenditures. Are you looking to expand brand awareness, find new customers, or engage with current customers to create better products? What kind of returns do you want? Tracking your success through social media metrics can be a complicated process, and one with many levels. By going in with a plan, and knowing what you want out of your efforts, you will create a better marketing approach.

The first set of data is straightforward and easy to measure. If you create a Facebook page, it can begin with how many friends you have after set benchmarks: Day One. Day 30. Three months out. After time, this growth may slow as you gather those users who are already loyal and excited to be part of your community.

The same can be said of the microblogging service Twitter— you may start out with large, rapid growth, which will eventually max out. While it can be rewarding to turn to coworkers and say, "We have 10,000 fans!" success can't be measured simply in the number of "friends" or "followers," both of which are presented clearly on the site itself for you and your customers to see. The next step is measuring their engagement.

Here, again, the services themselves provide some of this information for you. Wall posts and discussion comments on Facebook will suggest whether or not you're engaging with people on the site. Facebook's page site also shows how effective your page is, and offers suggestions for improvements.

Twitter mentions are another baseline indicator, which either come from retweets, when users repost what you've posted on their own feeds, or by brand mentions, designated by the "#" sign. The "#" symbol, or hashtag, as it's called, works as a signal that your Twitter post, or Tweet, is about a particular subject.

Frequency and use of the hashtag can be tracked using services such as Tweetdeck, Hootsuite and Monitter. Twitterholic can help you track the growth of your Twitter feed, Twitter search and Retweet can help you see how frequently you're mentioned, and Twitalyzer can help you parse the tone and frequency of your brand mentions and post effectiveness.

The same goes for virtually all web-based social networking applications: YouTube and Brightcove provide analytic data as well, while most blog services will provide some basic information about page views and users.

When it comes to more complex analysis, Google Analytics is still the top tool. The industry standard, this is a free service that enables you to track all sorts of information for your company's website. In order to use it, you have to be able to add the Analytics code to the code of your site (so it won't work on Twitter or Facebook—yet!), but it will work on any network your company develops and on your blogs.

Through Analytics, you can see who's coming to your site, where they're coming from, which search terms and keywords lead people to your site, where users are geographically, the time they spend on the site, how many and which links they follow, and lots of other useful information for web developers.

Being able to increase not only page views, but click-throughs and time on site, is useful for knowing what on your site is most engaging to your users. Google Analytics can also be incorporated with other sites—everything from the addition of Analytics to your browser's toolbar to combining with AdSense, Google's ad hosting software, to see how effective ad campaigns and conversions are.

Other sites, such as Digg and Stumbleupon, will show whether particular content on your site is popular within those communities, while Technorati will show something called "site authority," or basically, how strong your brand is on the Internet. The lower your "authority" number, the stronger your site.

All this raw data can show whether or not users are visiting and engaging with your site, but translating this into ROI can be difficult, though not impossible. For example, in June 2009, Dell reported $3 million in earnings directly through Twitter since 2007, when the company began tweeting discounts, promotions and new products on the site. Dell also reported $1 million earnings from Dell Outlet over a six-month period, directly attributable to customers who arrived on the site via Dell Outlet's Twitter account.

It may take time, for instance, for an increased web presence to clearly cause an increase in sales for some brands. Direct overlay of sales data can suggest such trends, as in the case of Dell. But the value of increased engagement on social media networks, as in any situation, may have other benefits. Customer satisfaction, trends in your industry or in press, and improved customer service can all come from such a presence.

On the other end—for seeing where and how your business and industry is viewed from the outside (e.g., your "buzz")—there are a number of products available. Social Mention, for instance, works like Google Alerts. Enter a search term, and the site will show you how and what information is being exchanged across social networks.

Trendrr, a real-time social media analytics platform, is a paid service used by public relations firms and advertising agencies, political campaigns, and corporate giants such as Microsoft and Verizon. Trendrr mines comprehensive online sources for trend data across more than 50 data sets (e.g., social networks, levels of influence, sentiment and more). These trends enable businesses to make business decisions based on a unique aggregation of relevant variables.

Radian 6, another paid service used by companies such as Pepsi, Dell and Comcast, offers real-time information, including highlighting "influencers" and goes beyond simple tracking to allow users to engage with customers throughout platforms.

Of course, there are paid services which will simplify the task even further for marketers—for a price. Omniture, by Adobe, offers a number of packages for data analysis, including recommendations for enhancements and improvements based on the data.

Nielsen's products, including NetRatings, BuzzMetrics and Analytic Consulting help sift through the information as well— they mine over 90% of worldwide Internet usage in order to find trends and best practices. For most companies, however, these services can be exceptionally cost-prohibitive.

Tools such as Trendpedia can be highly useful as well. A free tool that enables users to spot trends in social media by entering keywords and clicking "Search Trend," Trendpedia delivers blog articles in a trendline showing the popularity of a topic over time (currently, this tool tracks back only as far as three months).

This and other tools will enable you to not only benchmark your internal success, but also gauge your success against competitors by determining the level of buzz they are receiving and in which social networking spaces.

It's important to reiterate that measurement in the social media space takes on a different meaning than in other forms. Where we might have tracked success largely on volume in direct mail, in the social media space, success may look a lot smaller—but may include a core group of highly engaged consumers who are delighted to blog and tweet and create podcasts on behalf of your brand. Mission accomplished.

Depending on the size of your campaign and your budget, along with the proliferation of free services to track social networking metrics, the best choice may be to do it on your own. You know the needs of your company, and through the social networking sites and third-party applications like Google Analytics, you'll have all the information at hand to discover if you're meeting your goals and how to adapt your strategy as your web presence grows.

21

Bolster Your Special Forces Units

PUBLIC RELATIONS AND media relations have evolved
in dramatic ways with the advent of social media.
Corporate public relations has evolved from the days
of contacting a PR agent, pitching a story or sending in a video
news release (VNR) and hoping for a several-minute spot on the 6
o'clock news. Public relations continues to play an important role
in an organization's brand strategy, but some of a company's core
tasks in garnering PR have changed.

On the opposite end, companies need to pay closer attention
to how they are handling media relations, and in particular, their
online newsrooms, as these can be the make or break for media
outlets seeking access and assets. Companies who offer such
content-rich goodies as online photographs in low- and high-res;
click-throughs to schedule interviews with senior management,
requests for the expert and more—will clearly have the upper hand
when it comes to garnering coverage.

To the extent that you may be more or less familiar with the major shifts, we'll take you through the overarching tide changes in public/media relations as well as offer a word on investor relations.

THE NEW, OLD PUBLIC RELATIONS

In the dark ages—the last days of the 20th century—public relations obeyed strict rules to achieve fairly predictable outcomes.

Take press releases: Everybody in the business of attracting the press knew you only sent them out when you had "big news." No release was complete without a made-up, jargon-packed "quotation" attributed to the CEO—and don't forget that grip-and-grin photo with the giant fake check!

If you were lucky, reporters didn't toss your release in the trash (this was before recycling, remember?) Your job was "public relations," but you could only reach the public by going through those finicky, stressed-out gatekeepers, wading through waist-high stacks of hard-copy press kits. Talk about an exercise in cross-your-fingers-and-hope-for-coverage!

But on the other extreme, the advent of social media— Facebook, Twitter, LinkedIn, YouTube, blogs, wikis and more— has left many seasoned PR professionals wondering if their tactics are past their best-before date.

At the same time, print media is shedding subscribers, staff, stock value, credibility—and therefore, its gatekeeper role.

This means that instead of courting the media, every firm can, and must, become media. Social media sends messages around the world in moments, eliminating that Big Media middleman.

But bear in mind that social media culture rewards "dialogue," "conversation," "community" and other Kumbaya stuff that may set veteran PR flaks' teeth on edge.

However, this collaborative atmosphere works in the favor of anyone with a cause, product or service to promote. Ideally, followers and friends on Twitter and Facebook will become your "rabid fans" and spread your message. (This is more likely to happen if you adopt a "pull" strategy rather than a "push" one: for example, nine out of ten of your tweets should be either entertaining or informative; only one should push your "real" message.)

That said, traditional media is far from dead. Your old media contacts (what's left of them) are hanging out at Twitter and Facebook, so you should be, too.

Reporters add their social media contact information to sites like Muck Rack and MediaOnTwitter because they want to be found. Search for journalists by location or beat, and start following them on Twitter.

From a 2007 survey conducted by Bulldog Reporter and TEKgroup International on journalists and media relations practices:[1]

- Journalists' first choice for receiving news releases is via e-mail

- 77.9% of journalists prefer to receive news releases via e-mail

- 7.9% prefer commercial newswires

---

[1] Bulldog Reporter and TEKgroup, "2007 Journalist Survey on Media Relations Practices," (2007).

- 4.5% prefer online newsrooms

- Journalists continue to adopt social media

- Almost 70% of journalists read one or more blogs regularly

- Just over 28% visit social networking sites once per week or more

- More than 37% of journalists subscribe to RSS feeds

*Based on responses from 2,046 journalists

From this same report, came aggregate data on journalists and their use of online newsrooms:

- Nearly 50% of journalists visit online newsrooms more than once/week

- Over 73% visit online newsrooms more than once/week

- Importantly, almost 50% of journalists generally agree that it is often difficult to find an organizations' online newsroom

- Journalists use online news portals

- 50% of journalists visit Google News

- More than 30% of journalists visit Yahoo! News

• Journalists' usage of Google News surpasses their usage of major networks, such as MSNBC and CNN

The findings also reported what most public relations and corporate officials already know—that journalists remain skeptical of public relations—and thus, social media provides the perfect storm for public relations professionals to begin to reengage with a wary media in more collegial and meaningful interactions.

On the measurement side, the old public relations metrics were measured in clips: Print, television, radio and online. Beyond tracking these impressions, the impact could be difficult to ascertain. With the advent of social media, the new public relations metrics still include measuring the clips, but have expanded to include web traffic, page views/impressions, blog activity, links, SEO rankings and comments. For public relations professionals who have ever felt that the fruits of their labor were difficult to support in quantitative ways, you may rejoice at this plethora of methods for measuring the value of your work against an organization's bottom line—but only if you've planned to include these metrics in your strategy.

The reality is that public relations professionals, journalists and corporate communicators have more opportunities than ever before to engage with one another, and to provide value to one another. Some of the handiest sites for fostering this engagement are:

Help A Reporter Out (HARO)
http://www.helpareporter.com
Reporters submit queries to HARO for public relations professionals

Journalisted
http://www.journalisted.com
Currently, this site covers British media (plans are said to be in the works for a U.S. expansion). Users can search favorite reporters across 21 UK news outlets and 14 different websites, letting PR professionals read journalists' work before pitching them.

Media People Using Twitter
http://twitteringjournalists.pbworks.com/Media-People-Using-Twitter-Around-The-World
A wiki site featuring journalists who are active in Twitter

PitchEngine
http://blog.pitchengine.com/
Subscription-based site offers a host of Web 2.0 tools for creating Social Media Release (SMR) including links to social network profiles, video and photos. Reporters can subscribe to receive press releases via RSS feeds.

ReportingOn
http://reportingon.com
Enables reporters to discuss their stories or beats by answering the question, "What Are You Reporting On?" Reporters can tag their beat so PR pros can locate them easily—and they can seek out other journalists as resources.

Search.Twitter.com

http://search.twitter.com/

Produces less specific results for journalists, but still a great place to search corporate groups, pages and people via Search.Twitter. com

Twellow

http://www.twellow.com

Self-billed as the "Twitter Yellow Pages" this site categorizes users and enables searches on such category keywords as "journalist" or "public relations"

Susan Payton of Egg Marketing & Public Relations recommends interacting "with the journalist in her own space. I comment on posts I like. I retweet her content on Twitter. This way, by the time I'm ready to pitch her, I'm already on her radar."[2]

Requests for help are common on Twitter, especially when news is breaking: "I'm looking for someone to interview about..." Look for opportunities to send reporters a message like, "I see you've been writing about X. Can I send you info about a good resource?" (And use an ordinary @ tweet, not a direct message, or "DM"—they're considered too presumptuous for initial contacts.)

As far as professional public relations skills needed to succeed, these, too, have transformed in the wake of social media. In many respects, the work of the public relations professional has become more intense.

In addition to the baseline skills needed for this work (e.g., strong writing and communication skills, a knack for detail when

---

[2] Susan Payton, "HOW TO: Use Social Media in Your PR Pitch Plan" (Mashable the Social Media Guide, Blog, November 2009). http://mashable.com/2009/10/12/social-media-pr-pitch

it comes to content, and an ability to engage members of the media in a proactive and targeted way, today's public relations professional will need to add a set of online skills. This includes an understanding of blogs and microblogging and the importance of creating RSS feeds for content, along with pitching bloggers, basic knowledge of search-engine optimization and use of keywords and social media specific ethics to better approach situations such as astroturfing (creation of artificial buzz) and ghost tweeting or ghost blogging in the wake of authenticity.

Your recipe for the perfect Web 2.0 press release has evolved as well. You will want to continue to create both a standard version and a social media version, but your social media press release should contain core elements such as keywords—not buzzwords, a "What's-In-It-For-Me" subhead, an optional quote, as the canned one-liner is no longer a necessity, links, bookmarks, tags and additional resources designed to help journalists to tell your story.

Approaching traditional journalists through social media is easy. However, in 2009, pitching bloggers became a lot harder.

Before then, it wasn't uncommon for PR types to ask bloggers to review new products or services. Critics called this "payola," and the Federal Trade Commission (FTC) agreed. New regulations require bloggers to "disclose the material connections they share with the seller of the product or service" or face fines up to US$11,000.

However, opportunities for carefully crafted blogger endorsements will still exist. Jennifer Laycock of Search Engine Guide offers tips for pitching bloggers:[3]

---

[3] Jennifer Laycock, "5 Mistakes That Can Tank Your PR Pitch to Bloggers" (Search Engine Guide, August 2007). http://www.searchengineguide.com/senews/010431.html

1. Use the right name! "PR firms fail in this regard time and time again."

2. Don't lie about reading a blog. "If you don't read the blog, simply explain why you are targeting it. (e.g., 'We know that your blog is one of the most respected resources on Y.')"

3. Check to see if a blogger accepts pitches

4. Don't pitch irrelevant products

To generate buzz about a new cell phone application, Todd Defren at PR Squared created "unique angles and pitches for each and every blogger," written in distinct "voices."[4]

He reports, "In one month of blogger relations outreach, MobileSphere's slydial service was covered in 381 blog posts … The PR program helped boost slydial's 5,000 private alpha users to more than 200,000 beta users in less than two weeks."

The challenge of measuring return on investment (ROI) is one reason social media techniques aren't readily adopted. However, it is possible to measure success beyond just traffic spikes or numbers of "Diggs."

Social media consultant Jason Falls believes social media engagement pays off—because big companies have said so:

---

[4] Todd Defren, "Blogger Relations (and Social Media Release!) Case Study," (February 2009). http://www.pr-squared.com/2009/02/blogger_relations_and_social_m.html

"...look at the millions of dollars Marriott racks up from Bill Marriott's blog. Look at the sales Southwest Airlines attributes to its social media activity. Look at the $3 million Dell reported earning from its @delloutlet Twitter account. Look at Wiggly Wigglers, which has 90,000 worldwide customers, largely because when they talk about a product on their blog they put an 'order here' link along with it."[5]

Monitor your brand using tools like TweetDeck, eCairn, BuzzLogic, Reputation Defender and Hootsuite. (Google Alerts just aren't fast enough anymore!)

Dissatisfied customers are as likely to share a bad experience on Twitter as they are to phone customer service. And unlike that call to the 800 number, these reputation-killing anecdotes can go viral in minutes.

Two companies learned that the hard way. The Australian company Cotton On makes baby T-shirts with cheeky slogans. But some felt one slogan went too far. The company's "They Shake Me" tee—referencing shaken baby syndrome—prompted mommy bloggers to contact the company directly, while others complained on Twitter, writing posts like, "Cotton On thinks child abuse is funny."

"In this case," wrote marketing and social media guru David Meerman Scott, "Cotton On failed because company representatives did not send a tweet, nor did they comment on the blogs that were critical of the company's actions. Even just one tweet acknowledging the issue and pledging to look into it is better than no reaction at all."[6]

---

[5] Jason Falls, "Why Social Media Purists Won't Last," (November 2009). http://socialmediatoday.com/SMC/pages/print/posts/?bid=1236e02b-f349-4721-8aed-3747aa7b1d02&mode=Full
[6] David Meerman Scott, "Social media and the Cotton On baby T-shirt crisis," (September 2009). http://www.webinknow.com/2009/09/social-media-and-the-cotton-on-baby-tshirt-crisis-.html

Now Cotton On has the dubious distinction of being a case study on what not do in corporate social media.

From what babies wear, we move to moms wearing babies, and a very different corporate response to public upset. Unlike Cotton On, the makers of painkiller Motrin responded faster to a similar consumer backlash, sparked by an ad featuring moms using baby slings. The slings were compared to fashion accessories. Some felt the ad trivialized motherhood and took to Twitter to complain. Others posted parody ads and angry videos on YouTube. Perhaps of greatest concern was that close to 90% of the moms who tweeted an outcry hadn't even seen the original ad, but simply heard the story of the ad through fellow microbloggers.

The company sent an apology to bloggers, then posted it at Motrin.com, along with a vow to pull the ad. Ideally, Motrin would also solicit feedback on future ads from this passionate online (and no-cost) "focus group."

"E-eputation" control is harder than ever thanks to the web. Obviously, you can monitor comments on a company blog, but if you scrub "bad reviews" entirely, readers will sense that and respond accordingly.

Hence, part of your media strategy will also always be centered on reputation management. You will want to monitor your online reputation to find out what people are saying about your brand—or other key topics that may affect your brand. Your brand management also entails giving the brand a human face. Companies who have been wildly successful at this include Southwest Airlines, Zappos and Best Buy.

When faced with negative bloggers, you will want to contact them directly—by phone if you can—and try to resolve the situation diplomatically. Know, however, that bloggers typically will not take down old posts, so do not feel as though you have "lost" if this is the final answer.

Content positions your brand for the purpose of reputation management, enabling you to maximize the positive references about your brand by feeding search behemoths like Google with positive press, or simply blogging about exciting new product releases, talent hires or partnerships.

In promoting your company through positive content, your goal should be, in part, to weed out the "haters" and the competitors' comments—provided you aren't stripping away legitimate consumer complaints and concerns, which must not only remain, but must be addressed head on.

On the flip side of reputation management and media engagement, a well-crafted social media press release provides companies with a modicum of image control. Unlike old-fashioned press releases sent via fax or hard copy through the mail, those designed for and posted on the web will turn up in search engine results for years. So for those who have ever bemoaned the futility of the press release that came in with a whimper and left without a mention, we can all feel a little bit better.

A successful social media press release should focus not on the company, but on potential customers. The social media release should avoid trendy insider jargon, stressing instead popular keywords your ideal audience is already searching for. Gone are the days of public relations professionals writing for "AP" (Associated Press style)—now they are writing for "SEO." In this vein, you will also want to be sure to include anchor text and hyperlinks that lead back to your main site.

Once you have your release in hand (replete with targeted keywords), you will want to send press releases to the top wire services: PRWeb, PRNewswire, Businesswire, Weblogwire, Marketwire and PRXbuilder, among others.

Adam Singer of Top Rank suggests making that main site and/or a company blog the "centerpiece" of your strategy. Your tweets, keyword-rich online press releases, YouTube videos and other social media efforts will emanate from and/or point back to this main site.

Singer warns:

"Using Twitter or any network you don't control as the centerpiece is a mistake, because you're building the value of a digital asset that isn't really yours (no analytics, no control, no SEO benefit and if that network falls out of favor all your hard work is devalued)." [7]

Your site's online newsroom is equally important. Its search function must be robust, videos must start playing in seconds, and a real human being must be one or two clicks away, at most.

Nobody likes to fill out forms. Instead, offer RSS feeds or e-mail updates so reporters and customers can get fresh content delivered right away. Other must-haves include executive biographies, photos in various sizes, resolutions and file formats, and of course, links to all your other social media sites. Some additional recommendations for engaging with the media are:

• Like the dual strategy of the traditional and the social media press release, you will want to use a multi-tiered approach to media relations.

• Ensure that your news can be found in Google and Yahoo! search engines. Journalists are going to the same places we are

[7] Adam Singer, "Why Use Social Media For Public Relations" (Top Rank Online Marketing Blog, November 2009). http://www.toprankblog.com/2009/11/social-media-pr/

when it comes to keeping up with the news. Invest in SEO to be sure your item surfaces in these important sites.

• Given the understanding that journalists read and subscribe to blog RSS feeds, you will want to ensure that you are including items you wish to promote in your company's blog.

• Flexibility is your ally: Prepare company news in multiple formats—a press release, blog, update to your Facebook newsfeed, update on Twitter, etc.

• If you don't have a robust online newsroom, get one—and fast—and be sure it is easy to spot from your company's homepage. Gone are the days of burying the newsroom in the basement of your site.

• If you have been using a traditional wire service alone, this will no longer suffice. The goal today is to strike a balance between mass distribution and targeted messages to journalists who cover your industry.

• No spamming journalists, please. Eblasting your message is no different from the days of bombarding news organizations with faxed releases—only your eblast will be more invasive and even less welcome.

Social media is not a public relations quick fix. It takes time to build and maintain an online reputation, and effort to keep up with ever-changing best practices. However, public relations professionals can and must take ownership of social media tactics and strategies. The alternative is to be left further behind with every passing day, while competitors take the lead.

INVESTOR RELATIONS

Meanwhile, in the realm of investor relations, in July 2008, in a 47-page document, the SEC announced the recognition of corporate blogs as an official means of public disclosure.

The rules are straightforward, if not unsurprising, yet for companies who haven't stopped to consider which old rules apply to which new media, the top three rules that any company must adhere to are:

• Disclosure of material information must follow Regulation Fair Disclosure guidelines

• All social channels must be treated the same as traditional channels (disclosure controls)

• Only previously disclosed information should be shared

The risks that we are seeing companies experience, stem not from malicious intent, bur rather, from innocent updates posted in social networks, such as a senior official's blog, or a tweet about an upcoming product launch. For example, eBay launched a corporate blog featuring updates on conferences and quarterly earnings calls. Great idea, but until legal tapped them on the shoulder, they simply were not aware of the requirement to include regulatory disclaimers within certain posts. This is where mobilizing your "A Team" can really come in handy!

The conglomerate of public and investor relations, along with marketing, legal, human resources and corporate communications can work in a powerful and effective way to create awareness amongst all stakeholders (read: any employee who may have access to a computer and thus, social media). While this begins with a clear policy on social media, it continues through ongoing training.

But from an Investor Relations perspective, in which companies such as Chevron, Shell, Rio Tinto, UPS, Johnson & Johnson, Sun Microsystems and Barrick Gold are operating, suffice it to say that adaptations of IR rules must be taken into consideration.

22

Social Media Battle Stations— Your First Tour of Duty

"**O**KAY, GO!"
"Should I send it?"
"Yeah, just click 'update' already."
"Alright, I'm sending it…here we go. It's there, it's posted!"

Sound familiar? We hear this a lot. It's the ritual conversation that seems to occur prior to our clients' sending up their first exciting tweets into the Twittersphere. It's usually followed by applause and cheering on the level of Neil Armstrong's walk on the moon.

Most companies will feel giddy at first at their initial outreach in social media. This is soon followed by anticipation and perhaps a bit of angst, as they ponder whether anyone will notice and if they notice, how they will respond.

"We've been retweeted! We got three retweets!" More applause. The newly minted tweeters and bloggers are still excited, still hopeful, but may not be sure where these small signs of life may lead. If properly cultivated, they will lead to bigger and better brand equity, but in order to reach that goal, create a plan based on the following:

Start small. Web 2.0 has given rise to a plethora of highly attractive networks, sites and applications, numbering in the thousands—and growing. Begin with one core site (up to three if you are well-resourced) that your staff can dedicate its efforts to and evolve from there.

Sign up for accounts, and create pages on Facebook and Twitter. Also consider MySpace (despite it's slow to stagnating growth in subscriber rate, this network remains a viable and important network, not to be underestimated or excluded from your social media planning).

Determine the types of content you will post and the frequency for each element (e.g., blog once a week; tweet 3-5 times per day; post Facebook updates on Mondays, Wednesdays and Fridays). Keeping content fresh and lively is the trick to establishing and sustaining interest. If your plan is to post frequently, be sure you are not simply tweeting to tweet, but that your content is substantive and relevant.

Understand the demographics of each network you are planning to enter, and be sure to take this into account as you are planning your editorial calendar. Useful, on-the-spot information tends to work best, so offer tips, time-savers, sneak previews or pre-sale announcements as a means of getting audiences into the habit of identifying your sites with real value.

While customers know you have a product or service to sell, avoid pitching and selling ad nauseam as this defeats the purpose of social media, which is to create two-way conversation as opposed to one-way promotion. An ongoing infomercial disguised as a blog or a Facebook account is the quickest way to lose your potential base.

And hardest of all, be patient. Building awareness, driving traffic and creating active engagement takes time. You may feel as though your efforts equate to whistling in the wind. But if you are persistent—and consistent—with solid, interesting, substantive content posted at frequent intervals, you will see pickup as word spreads.

Many clients going into social media want a definitive response to the question of time commitment. This is likely a question you've been asking yourself as you consider your staff and the seemingly overwhelming resource demands that your organization continues to face. Sometimes extremes can offer perspective. For example, founder of Engadget and mega-blogger Peter Rojas is famous for spending 80 hours per week blogging—but he also turned his technology blog into one of the most-read in the blogosphere. Most companies are looking just to incorporate some core elements of social media into our everyday marketing and communications.

So, how much of a commitment are we really talking about? Like everything else, initially, the bulk of the time commitment will be spent determining the scope and skill set of those on your staff, marrying these up with your business objectives, and then ensuring that staff members are armed with a clear set of expectations and a tactical plan for getting there.

Let's say, for example, you have two overworked, underpaid staff members who will now need to add social media to their already stretched bandwidth. One blog post per week, a couple of daily tweets on Twitter and routine updates on Facebook and LinkedIn could become fairly nominal additions to their schedules. The key is in understanding the value of these applications in relation to your goals.

If being timely is important, and you are an organization that has acute news and updates to deliver, you'll want to devote your energies to Twitter. Even this can be once a day, or once every few days, when updates to the public are needed. Once you are comfortable in the space, this can literally be a five-minute task.

And keep in mind that tweeting for no reason can become a case of crying wolf. Take into consideration the reaction you will receive to steady, everyday tweets and be certain that this ongoing stream won't work against you when you really want to gain the public's attention. Too much tweeting can have the opposite effect in which followers grow tired of tweet after incessant tweet from your brand—and lose interest entirely. Everything in moderation.

The answer to "How long is this going to take?" will vary across organizations, like every other element of social media, but an ongoing presence doesn't have to take over your day, by any stretch. In fact, you'll want to start out devoting perhaps half an hour per day seeding content in key applications. Gauge the response and turn your time up or down accordingly.

Don't let the threat of another task wanting a piece of your time scare you off. Remember, you don't have to swallow the whole social media pie in one sitting. Creating a presence with a few core tools is the best way to establish a baseline for balancing your workload and forging ahead in the new media space.

Like anything else—making a major purchase, going from brunette to blonde, or ordering a case of the latest boutique wine— testing is always the most prudent first step.

As you are shaping your social media engagement strategy, consider what you will track as a measure of success. For example, with e-mail marketing campaigns, we are scanning the results for such important pieces of data as optimal day of the week and time of day to send for the highest open rate.

As you are setting up your social media campaign (and particularly, if you haven't entered this space before), consider your most informed guesstimate of the optimal time that users might engage. To arrive at your best guess, we recommend that you begin by doing some research into when your customer group (or a like customer group) appears active on the social networks in which you will attempt to engage them.

If you have a track record of days/times from other types of online campaigns, what information might this data provide? Visit competitor brands who may have already launched social media campaigns, and seek out patterns of activity (e.g., what day/time of day are blog comments and retweets occurring? If you have no competitor doing what you are planning to do, visit Trendrr (http://www.trendrr.com), which can provide you with valuable baseline information to at least head you down the right path.

Importantly, have a clear goal in mind for social media, understand your audience and its receptivity before you attempt to engage, and keep transparency at the forefront of your content creation. For a while Britney Spears told fans she was tweeting her own tweets, a fact that was met with skepticism, particularly from the die-hard fans. Finally, Britney came clean to reveal that staff members were posting the tweets. The fans and followers were fine with the still-close connection—and the honesty that came with it.

Guy Kawasaki also has a team of Twitterers, but unlike Britney, Guy was open about who was doing the tweeting at the onset.

Fans and consumers don't mind that you're not spending your day tweeting—but they do mind feeling duped.

Define criteria for success before you click "publish" or "post." The line between success and failure can be a fine one at first, so know what success looks like up front. Many companies falsely assume they are still dealing in quantity alone—and thus, the acquisition of just 500 followers on Twitter may seem disheartening.

But if these are the right 500 followers—brand advocates and ambassadors; your most loyal supporters—then adding 5,000 lukewarm, disinterested, or worse yet, disgruntled followers may not spell greater success. Rather, it might spell disaster if you are not prepared to handle negative engagement.

23

Your Network or Theirs?

W ITH THE FLOOD of competition on the social networking giants like Facebook and MySpace, it can be useful to pull away from the crowd and create a social network exclusively for your brand. There are many advantages, some pitfalls, and lots of tools to help marketers do this, but there are also a few important aspects to keep in mind.

What benefit, specifically, do you want your brand to see by entering social networking? If you are looking for a simple presence, then joining an existing service might make the most sense. Your customers are familiar with the interface and have to provide little effort in engaging with your brand. A fan site or page on Facebook is, for many users, an expected minimum these days, and even if you decided to build your own, some sort of presence on the site lends legitimacy to your goals.

With Facebook, many of the tools you want in order to engage with customers and allow them to communicate with you are available and simple to use. Plus, each connection is a valuable one. Each time a fan of your page commits some kind of action—leaves a comment or "likes" a post—it shows up on their friends' news feeds as well: common and constant advertising and C2C branding. Nearly every major brand has an existing Facebook page.

Many have done an admirable job—some focusing on consumer needs and customer interaction, others using it as a brand extension to deliver content. Southwest Airlines asks customers on the site what could make their flying experience better and are quick to respond to complaints on their Facebook wall. Integration of brand-specific applications, which require the work of a software developer, can further strengthen your identity on the site and help your brand stand out. Dominos Pizza created a Facebook application which allows users to track their order on Facebook and share the information with their friends—not only providing a service to the customer, but illustrating one of Domino's key branding points—quick delivery.

Facebook, with its popularity, is a clear choice and even a requirement of brands. But there is a lot of information on the site, and it's easy to get lost in the mix, especially for companies with a smaller profile. Joining existing niche social networking sites can provide the more specific pool of customers your company is looking for. BlackPlanet, focused on the African American market, has many of the same features as Facebook, while LinkedIn, a site for professionals to network, can help a B2B business thrive. But many smaller communities have their own sites as well, and depending on your brand, sites like gamerDNA, for video game enthusiasts, or GoodReads, for avid readers, will help you reach new customers. If your brand is in line with a niche site, engaging with those users can reap great rewards.

Another option, though, is crafting your own social network. The level of complexity is up to you, as well as the form the sites take. Companies from Coca Cola to Nike to Bank of America have social networking elements in their sites. It can range from an option like MyCokeRewards, which allows users to accrue points from bottle tops for branded merchandise and content offerings, to Bank of America's small business network, which allows small businesses to create profiles, communicate with each other, and form mentorships, all while engaging with Bank of America's product offerings.

For other brands, social networking has become part of their identity. This strategy is particularly powerful for online services. Amazon.com's lists, allow users to create lists of suggestions for purchase based on a theme, like "Kitchen Must-Haves" and "Best Books of the Year." Here social networking, branding and sales meld perfectly: the consumers become the trusted source for other consumers in a non-intrusive way. Netflix, famous for its suggestion algorithm for choosing DVDs of interest to consumers, also has a well-crafted social-networking element, where users can choose to share the films they've ordered with their friends on the site. Netflix also integrates this with its Facebook presence, using an application to allow customers to share DVD choices as status updates.

Meanwhile, content providers allow users to set up profiles to share favorite content, comment and exchange with other users. It increases time-on-site and pageviews, while strengthening the loyalty of users on the site. Sites from MTV.com to CNN.com allow users to create logins and become part of the community—

while reaping the benefits of user-generated content as well. Even a basic login-based system, allowing shared wish lists or content sharing, can be a goldmine for marketers.

Not only does it create and solidify a consumer base, it provides marketers with a huge amount of specific information about users, all of it customizable. Age, location, income, preferences and movement on the site can all be collected with this basic level of social networking.

There are many programs allowing marketers and developers to create these social networks. Ning, one such service, uses fully customizable CSS and third-party developers for maximum flexibility. Creation of a basic network is ad supported, while a fee can allow more control over information. A Ning network can be invite-only, great for an employee-based network, or can be open to anyone. You can also control whether or not your network shows up in web searches.

KickApps, another service program, allows an even deeper customization and integration with your current website for seamless branding and offers price packages based on usage. Both sites host your information for you, which is an advantage if you're a small business with data storage concerns. If, however, you need to be able to host your own information, you'll need a different solution.

Crowd Factory is a site which allows a company to store information on its own servers and provides full-service crafting— working with your web developers, they can create an integrated network for your site. Comcast.com and Martha Stewart both use Crowd Factory software. LiveWorld is another network system with full-customization which leaves content in the hands of the company. Some of its current clients include Campbell's Soup and American Express.

This option, which leaves companies with the greatest amount of control over look and feel, as well as information on the site, can be expensive, with some packages costing over $50,000. That can be a big risk if you're not sure how your customers will respond to the service. Users need a reason to join a new social network, and no one wants to be the only person on a site.

In the end, it's best to choose the service that most closely aligns with your needs as an organization, while allowing room to grow. Facebook and other existing sites are familiar to users, attract new customers while solidifying relationships with current customers, and allow for cross-platform support. Tailored and customized networking sites allow for more control on the part of the customer and creative interactions, all while maintaining a brand image. There is no reason not to engage with the existing sites—they are inexpensive and easy to use—but creative approaches, from an Amazon.com model to Bank of America's small business network, can add a new level of engagement with your customers.

24

Navigate Your Risk

AMIDST WHAT SHOULD decidedly be your excitement about launching a social media campaign on behalf of your brand, should be some words of caution to ensure against failing within this space and inadvertently causing your brand more harm than good.

Some surefire ways to fail include: Jumping into social media without a plan; failing to listen to target audiences and failing to hone in on sites, tools and applications they are using; creating first and planning later (e.g., many companies create a Facebook page or Twitter account, then sit back and wait for traffic...which never comes); failing to provide strong, targeted content; failing to create basic policies or offering poor customer service (e.g., setting the expectation of active engagement, and then taking too long to respond, not responding at all, etc.). Another culprit that many companies inadvertently fall victim to is the big bang, sudden stop (e.g., Victoria's Secret "PINK" Campaign on Facebook, which garnered great interest and appeal. When the campaign was over, however, the company had no rollover plan, so simply closed up shop, leaving engaged consumers to wonder where they went).

While social media can explode your business by creating positive, viral exposure at a rapid rate, it can backfire on a company that is not clear on its objective, its audience, its message—or all three. The result is that this can be the fastest way to lose control of your brand.

Other consequences that may be less than stellar? Nothing happens. An example of launching a campaign to almost sub-zero response is Jenny Craig's Facebook page, Wikipedia entry and blog. In addition, WeightWatchers' now infamous three-tweet special (in February 2009, Weight Watchers launched a Twitter account, tweeted three times, and seemingly abandoned the effort). Again, dragging your brand out into the middle of town for public humiliation is never the goal.

More risks abound for those who aim to pose or ghost blog. Cruise Critic blog positioned itself as an objective observer of all things cruises, but was later publicly outed when it was discovered that the blog owner was actually a company owned by Expedia. This prompted a series of highly negative response postings (e.g., "Royal Caribbean caught infiltrating review sites with viral marketing team"), which will now be floating out in the digital space for—well, likely for forever—or until Web 3.0 comes along and wipes Web 2.0 off the face of the map. It didn't help that travel great Arthur Frommer was part of the public voice questioning the value of user reviews and user-generated content in the wake of this sham.

More opportunity that awaits a brand in social media is expanded reach to potential target audiences, but this comes with the cost of investing time, energy and money. Being on hand in this space to defend yourself and your brand (crisis management) and being able to take control of public perception of your brand (positioning and reputation management) are two more criteria for the plus side, while the downside is opening yourself up to criticism—and learning to let it ride and instead of scrubbing it away, addressing it with your publics. This one can be a hard one to swallow, particularly for those companies who are inclined to be perfectionists when it comes to brand representation.

Negative posts, tweets and comments can and will occur—even as a brand attempts to create engagement opportunities for its target audiences. For instance, Skittles launched an interactive "Taste the Rainbow" campaign, and while they did receive consumer response, it was not what the brand had bargained for. The contest took a nosedive after being met with raunchy comments, to the point where the site simply had to be taken down. Unknown variables such as these can be hard to control for.

And then, of course, the publishers themselves can make big mistakes, such as Lance Armstrong and his public smack-talking comment about his Tour de France-winning teammate, Alberto Contador. Verizon's policy blog editor sent a tweet pertaining to the site of AT&T's major conference showing a photo of a Verizon truck parked outside of the facility in which AT&T's conference was being held. His commentary read:

> "This is what USA's most reliable wireless network sends BEFORE a conference."

While the comment was not libelous, still, a rubbing-it-in-your-face positioning from the policy blog editor within a company may create undesired consequences in terms of overall brand position-ing.

Know these risks and rewards up front, and you'll be better armed for success.

25

Social Media Wasteland

THE ONSLAUGHT OF SOCIAL MEDIA sites has created a growing problem of social media blight: Company Facebook pages that lie dormant. Branded Twitter feeds with nary a tweet. Corporate social networks without return visitors. These wastelands are missed opportunities to connect with consumers and red flags that the company isn't paying attention.

A study of Fortune 100 companies conducted in the summer of 2009 by communications firm Burson-Marsteller with Proof Digital found that while their involvement in Twitter and Facebook is widespread, 31 percent of the Twitter accounts tweeted less than three times a week and 28 percent of the Facebook fan pages had little or no comments, few if any postings, and no indication that the page was being actively managed by the company.[1]

A separate study released in late 2009 paints a bleaker picture. The public relations firm Weber Shandwick estimated that 73 of

---

[1] "Burson-Marsteller and Proof Digital Fortune 100 Social Media Study," (The Burson-Marsteller Blog, July 31, 2009).
http://www.burson-marsteller.com/Innovation_and_insights/blogs_and_podcasts/BM_Blog/Lists/Posts/Post.aspx?ID=128

the Fortune 100 companies have registered a total of 540 Twitter accounts. More than half (52 percent) of those accounts were not actively engaged, as measured by number of links, hashtags, references and retweets.

Fifteen percent of the accounts were inactive; of those, 11 percent were placeholder accounts used to protect corporate names from brandjacking (see for example, MonsterJobs, where 169 followers wait vainly for a signal). Another 4 percent were simply abandoned.[2]

The problem is exacerbated by imposter accounts. Dell, Volkswagen, Nike and Adobe are among the corporations that don't own their brand names on Twitter.[3] As a result, interested consumers are unwittingly tuning into a brand message controlled by someone else.

Exxon Mobil Corp. learned last year that people were paying attention to it even though it wasn't paying attention to them. Someone was impersonating a company representative under a Twitter account called ExxonMobileCorp. "Janet" seemed official; she reportedly fielded questions about the oil company's strategic direction and its philanthropy. She even addressed the Valdez oil spill—with the less-than-sensitive remark that while the spill was tragic, it wasn't among the top 10 such incidents.

The situation was a wake-up call to Exxon Mobil. "[You] need to be diligent about what is being said about you, by you, and those pretending to be you," Exxon spokesperson Alan Jeffers told blogger Jeremiah Owyang in an interview.[4] "Janet" has since parked her account, and now the company is tweeting regularly

---

[2] Weber Shandwick, "Do Fortune 100 Companies Need a Twittervention?" (November 2009). http://www.webershandwick.com/resources/ws/flash/Twittervention_Study.pdf
[3] Rupal Parekh, "GM, Kellogg, Nestle Beat to the Tweet as Squatters Take Over Twitter Names," (Advertising Age, November 9, 2009). http://adage.com/digital/article?article_id=140377
[4] Jeremiah Owyang, "How "Janet" Fooled the Twittersphere (and me) She's the Voice of Exxon Mobil," (Web Strategy, August 1, 2008). http://www.web-strategist.com/blog/2008/08/01/how-janet-fooled-the-twittersphere-shes-the-voice-of-exxon-mobil/

under the handle Exxonmobil, from a page emblazoned with corporate advertising with a direct link to the company.

Another squatter has the Apple account. There, would-be followers of the computer company encounter dead silence. More than 1,766 people have signed up to follow Apple, which to date has posted only a single tweet, "I love apples."[5]

Imposters and brand duplication are also a major problem on Facebook, which now has 1.4 million fan pages, according to the company. Missed opportunities and brand confusion are rife. Fans of DreamWorks Animation, for instance, will find two very legitimate-looking pages on Facebook. Unfortunately for the real DreamWorks, the imposter has five times as many fans.[6] Goldman Sachs isn't on Facebook, but the 5,000 fans on its unofficial page don't know that. The imposter page has been up at least since 2007 and hasn't posted a thing in years.

Official pages fall victim to neglect all the time. One company guilty of setting-it-and-forgetting-it is Cigna. The Philadelphia-based health care company created a page to promote a health-related e-learning series. More than a year and a half later, the site had more than 1,700 fans but not a single post or comment after the initial welcome.

Companies venturing into this space need to be vigilant, vocal and frequent. They should help users verify corporate identities by including advertisements and contact information with a phone number, just as corporate websites do. Internal social media policies should set guidelines for how and if employees can use the corporate name and logo in social networks so that unofficial sites are kept to a minimum.

---

[5] Willis Wee, "10 Brands Claimed By Twitter Cybersquatters," (September 21, 2009). http://www.penn-olson.com/2009/09/21/10-brands-claimed-by-twitter-cybersquatters/
[6] The official DreamWorks Animation page can be found at http://www.facebook.com/dreamworksanimation.

And when maintaining an account becomes too big of a job, the best thing to do is simply remove it. Utility company PECO removed its (inactive) Facebook page, PECO Philadelphia, after deciding that managing the site presented a daunting task it wasn't yet willing to undertake. The company is developing a social media strategy before it ventures out again.

With the difficulties of controlling the brand message on independent networks like Facebook and Twitter, many companies have simply built their own social communities. These sites typically have a flurry of new members at the beginning, but where they go from there depends on how well they keep members coming back.

Sites that don't create mutual purpose quickly turn to seed. Eleven months after MGM Grand at Foxwoods launched its social network, not a single group or forum discussion had been created. Of the 10 groups there, three actively undermined the brand, or would if anyone ever saw their posts. "My Clothes All Smell Like Nasty Cigarette Smoke" says one member. Two of the groups promote a totally unrelated company, Apple Computer Inc., with one group called "Why Macs are cool."[7]

Many communities have come and gone. Walmart's The Hub network, launched in the summer of 2006 ostensibly so teens would have a place to express their individuality, was derided in the blogosphere for its exclamation-point-laden youthful patois, rules that prevented members from e-mailing each other, and notification system that alerted parents when their kids join. The site was doomed to alienate the teenagers it was intended for, and it was shuttered after 10 weeks.[8] Reuters AdvicePoint, a financial adviser community that used direct marketing to invite investors to

---

[7] The site is at http://connect.mgmatfoxwoods.com
[8] Mya Frazier, "Wal-Mart Shuts Down the Hub: Retailer's Foray Into Social Networking Closes After Less Than Three Months," (Advertising Age, October 4, 2006).

"claim their profile," was replaced with a page stating that Reuters is reevaluating the service. EcoTreadsetters was a community built around environmentalism and tires by Yokohama Tire Corp. When it was launched in late 2007, the tire manufacturer issued a self-important invitation stating that it had decided "it was time that everyone became more concerned about the environment." But many people had been concerned for some time, and were already using sites like TreeHuggers, GreenBiz and Care2.

In late 2009, a group of researchers at ComBlu, a division of HLB Communications that builds online social communities, joined 135 corporate-built social communities belonging to Fortune 500 companies. They registered as users, created profiles and got set to engage.

They classified nearly a quarter of the communities as ghost towns.[9]

Not surprisingly, the health care industry, which faces regulatory scrutiny if social media users "report" adverse side effects on blogs or in networks, scored lowest overall for its social media engagement. But a number of entertainment companies did poorly as well. Sony's music site MyPlay, for example, attracts thousands of visitors, but didn't impress the researchers when it came to engagement. The vast majority of visits were one-time passers-by who rarely or never return, according to Quantcast analytics.

"I believe that truly the impact is that it represents a company's or brand's lack of engagement competency that they're missing the big opportunity to engage and build long-term relationships with their constituents," said Kathy Baughman, founder of ComBlu. "They are allowing competitors to engage in a way that can bring

---

[9] ComBlu, "The State of Online Branded Communities," (December 2009).
http://comblu.com/news/social-media/the-state-of-online-branded-communities.aspx

them over into their camp. That's the biggest danger and there's a real potential financial impact."

26
Your Social Media Marching Orders

FTER TRAVELING THROUGH This guide, you may feel as though all of this sounds like an awful lot of work. It is. And you may feel as though you will wait a bit longer before entering the space. You can. But know that social media has embedded itself, not in the minds of technology geeks or marketers, but in the minds of consumers who are finding the same types of value they discovered with e-mail and the Internet. So, your brand can't afford to sit this one out.

Organizations—any organization—all organizations—your organization—must pay attention to social media, or the brand you represent is at risk. Perhaps you think your social media efforts will never get off the ground because they will be drowned out in all the clutter of others who have already embraced social media tactics. Or you are still convinced that your brand will be damaged if you lose control of your message to the masses of consumers—or even competitors. Your brand is being damaged each time you ignore a comment on a blog about your product—so you might as well begin to pay attention. As for competition, social media brings a whole new outlook to this area as well, showing marketers that it's better to embrace them than to fear them (e.g., Pepsi tweets to Coke).

Remember that today's consumers don't get mad—they post on YouTube. Hence, your best practices in social media should mirror best practices in traditional media—only with some important twists. They are premised on the fact that the user must first understand how to initiate and manage a social media strategy, particularly when it comes to integration and alignment within the crosshairs of traditional marketing and communications plans. To recap:

• Match social media strategies with overall corporate strategies and objectives

• Develop and understand how social media networks work

• Assess resources, roles and responsibilities (e.g., community manager, corporate social media strategist)

• Engage outside help as necessary

• Determine metrics of success based on individual goals

• Develop a process for analysis and assessment

When planning and executing, think through your strategy via the lens of your consumer. Who is your ideal customer? When it comes to positioning, what do you want them to think about when they consider your brand? Know your target audience and their digital behavior. Are they really using Twitter? Prioritize your tactics to test based on digital behavior and your Most Wanted Response (MWR). Test constantly like a direct marketer, by tuning in to media outlets, platforms, ad creative, offers and landing pages. And try a range of outreach—from blogs to e-mail, to widgets, podcasting, video and social networks—yours and theirs.

Ultimately, what we know about corporate applications of social media is this:

- It can't make you smarter when it comes to doing the right thing

- It can make you smarter when it comes to listening to your clients and customers

- It is a powerful tool for tapping into your consumer base in unprecedented ways to elicit rapid communications, evaluations, iterations and actions

- Your strategy must be long term, even as technologies evolve and devolve at a frantic pace

- There is still much to learn in the social media realm

- Rules of traditional media still apply

- Social media, done right, is not a one-off campaign by a handful of staff; it's a corporate commitment.

Chances are high that you won't get everything right the first time. But you will gather important knowledge that will fuel the next iteration of your social media plan. The key is not to chase down every new application as it comes along, but rather to select a few core tactics based on your company's objectives, understand them thoroughly, implement them with precision, and analyze your results.

If executed well, your social media strategy will not only enhance your company's bottom line, it will alter how core audiences perceive your brand—and how the company perceives itself. Hence, anyone in a position to market, create buzz, or communicate out on behalf of a brand should feel supercharged by the landscape of opportunity that exists through the auspices of social media.

SURVIVAL KIT

Glossary of Terms

YOUR FIRST STOP in social media is at understanding the terms. The list below, while far from complete, will give you the basic terminologies and a number of stable applications that appear to be sticking around, at least at the time of this writing. Some applications will retain more traction than others, but all are an important part of the ongoing chronicles of social media: and what you'll need to know as you navigate the new media terrain.

@—Tag to use to refer to another social networking site user. (For example on Twitter: @username means either sending a message to "Username" or talking about "Username" in your message. On Facebook: by using the @username tag in one's status message, @ username is tagged and "@ username" becomes clickable to that user's profile page.)

AdSense—Google's contextual advertising program in which website owners can enable text and image advertisements based on the user's geographical location and other factors, on their sites. These ads are administered by Google and generate revenue on a per-click basis. http://www.google.com/adsense/

AdWords—A Google service that accepts advertisements for placement with Google search results and on others' websites. Advertisers pay Google for this service, and Google shares this revenue with the other website owners who publish these ads (via AdSense). http://www.google.com/adwords/

AJAX—Asynchronous JavaScript and XML. A group of interrelated web development techniques used on the client side to create interactive web applications or rich Internet applications that can retrieve data from servers asynchronously in the background without interfering with the display and behavior of the existing page.

Akismet—A spam filtering service created by Automattic. Akismet is used to filter link spam from blog comments and then applies those rules to block future spam. http://akismet.com/

API—Application Programming Interface. A set of routines, protocols and tools that software programmers can leverage to build software applications. APIs are useful because they eliminate the need for every application to be built from scratch.

Astroturfing—The artificial creation of a grassroots buzz for a product or service. Astroturf marketers typically use blogs, message boards, podcasts, wikis, vlogs, chat rooms and social media websites (such as MySpace and Facebook) when building an artificial buzz about a product or service.

Autoresponder—An e-mail utility that automatically replies to an e-mail message with a set reply when an e-mail arrives at a certain address. (Examples: "Out of office" reply that can be set up when an individual is on vacation or confirmation of subscription to a newsletter).

Authenticity—The quality of being genuine or "real," which in social media is at the center of effective communication. In many regards, authenticity has become the new institutional voice.

Avatar—A user's representation of himself, herself or an alter ego used to represent the individual social media profiles, online forums, communities and online computer games.

Badge—Icons used on a user's blog, website or profile to promote and interact with other social media websites. For example, a "Follow me on Twitter" icon or a "Facebook profile" icon on a blog will allow readers to easily interact with the blogger through other social media avenues, thus broadening and deepening the engagement.

Banner Ad—A form of advertising on the Internet that entails embedding an advertisement into a webpage. The banner ad is designed to attract traffic to a website by linking to the landing page or website of the advertiser.

Bebo—A social networking website that allows users to share a profile (either publicly or only with their friends) and connect with other users online. http://www.bebo.com/

Bing—Microsoft's search engine, originally created to focus on four verticals: making a purchase decision, planning a trip, researching a health condition and finding a local business. http://www.bing.com/

Bit.ly—A service that allows users to shorten, share and track URLs. Users are able to track unique visitors to their sites along with location and metadata of the visitor. http://bit.ly/

Blip.tv—A web service that allows independent content creators to upload their content to the site, offering free hosting and distribution to a large audience. Additionally, the service features optional advertising with a revenue share model. http://blip.tv/

Blog—To write or edit a shared online journal or an online user-published article.

Blogger—An individual who updates or maintains a blog.

Bloglines—An online service for searching, subscribing, creating and sharing news feeds, blogs and rich web content. The system aggregates content in a single location enabling the user to create a personalized news feed. http://www.bloglines.com/

Blogosphere—The space encompassing all blogs and their interconnections with one another.

Blogroll—A list of blogs, usually placed in the sidebar within a blog, that reads as a list of recommendations by the bloggers of other blogs.

Blogswarm—The situation in which large numbers of bloggers comment on the same story or news event. A blogswarm can become the "hot topic" of the day in the blogosphere.

Buzz—Anything that creates excitement or stimulates conversation in the social media space. Ideally, this involves influencers in the online community (defined by being authentic and having a following) who help to spread information and content through their online networks. Online discussion that mentions a brand in a positive light is the ideal buzz that companies aim to achieve.

Cloud Computing—A term used to describe the delivery of hosted services or resources over the Internet that are virtual and scaleable and take the place of the traditional requirement of a physical infrastructure.

Cloud Tag—Also called a word cloud or tag cloud. A visual representation of user-generated content tags with the popularity of the tag depicted by bolder, larger font than less popular tags.

Comments—User-generated content that expresses one's personal opinion or belief on everything from blogs, profiles and online forums, to products, services and sites by posting in response to already existing content.

Community—A social group whose members share a common interest, locality or function that brings members together.

Content—Information designed to provide value for an end user or audience in specific contexts. Content may be text, images, audio or video.

Content Aggregator—An individual or application that gathers web content from different sources for reuse or resale into a single platform.

Content Sharing—The sharing of information, photographs, music and videos via the Internet. Common content sharing sites include YouTube, Photobucket, Vimeo and Flickr.

Conversation—An informal exchange of ideas between two or more parties. Most social networking sites provide tools such as instant messenger, e-mail, forums and profile comments that allow users to communicate with one another.

Co-Tweet—A Twitter client focused on corporate Twitter customers to monitor, manage, aggregate and leverage Twitter from across multiple accounts and multiple Twitter users. http://cotweet.com/

Crowdsourcing—The application of tapping into the collective intelligence of public opinion to complete business-related tasks that a company would normally either perform itself or outsource (e.g., engaging with members of an existing social network to seek out fans to help solve problems, offer new ideas, etc.).

Daylife—A media services company that offers tools for content aggregation to be used on the user's website. Daylife maps connections between content by topic, country, geography and medium. http://www.daylife.com/

Delicious—A social bookmarking service that allows users to tag, save, manage and share web pages from a centralized source. http://delicious.com/

Digg—A social news website that allows users to contribute content and "dig" (vote) on the submitted links and stories. Content with the highest popularity is filtered to the front page of the site. http://digg.com/

Direct Message (DM)—A private message sent on Twitter from one Tweeter to another. Direct messages can be sent only to those who have elected to follow the sender.

Domain Name—A unique web address for an Internet site. The domain name can map to one or multiple IP addresses. (Example: In http://www.google.com, "google" is the domain name.)

Facebook—A social networking site focused on tools that help people communicate easily with one another. http://www.facebook.com/

Facebook Developer Platform—Standards-based web service with methods for accessing and contributing Facebook data. The platform is meant to encourage developers to create applications to help people communicate with one another. http://developers.facebook.com/

Feed—A web feed. This is a data format used for providing subscribers with the most up-to-date content available for the given search criteria.

Feedback Loop—A circular event in which the output from an event affects the input for another event in the future. (Example: in e-mail marketing, individuals can mark e-mail messages as spam and forward the e-mail for removal from the system.)

Feedburner—A web-based feed management provider (acquired by Google) that helps bloggers, podcasters and commercial publishers promote, deliver and profit from

their content on the Web. http://www.feedburner.com/

Flickr—An online image and video hosting website that seeks to allow users to easily share content (videos and photos) with the rest of the online community. Users are then able to comment on and tag the content. http://www.flickr.com/

Folksonomy—The practice of collaboratively creating and managing tags to annotate and categorize content.

Followers—Twitter users who have elected to receive another user's tweets (e.g., Twitter updates of those an individual is following will appear on the user's Twitter home page). Popularity on Twitter can be measured in part by the number of followers a person (or account) has.

Following—The collective group of followers a Twitter user has.

Forum—An online discussion site or message board.

Friending—The act of inviting someone to be a friend on a social networking site. That person can then accept or reject the friend request. On most social networking sites users cannot see a person's profile page until they have become "friends."

Friendster—A social networking site focused on tools to help users communicate easily with one another. Includes fan pages and a Friendster Developer Program. http://www.friendster.com/

Google Alerts—A service offered by Google that sends a daily e-mail to users notifying them of any updates that surface in Google search for the topic or keywords they have identified. For example, a company can have an alert for a CEO's name to become aware of content as it emerges. http://www.google.com/alerts

Google Analytics—A free service offered by Google that provides daily metric usage and analytical reports for visits to the subscriber's webpage. Users subscribe to the service and include a tag on their site in order to collect the necessary information about site visitors for analysis. http://www.google.com/analytics

Google Reader—A feed reader capable of reading RSS and Atom feeds. Users can manage feeds, label them and even share feed collections with others. http://www.google.com/reader

Hashtag (#)—A way to group topics on Twitter by including the # sign (hashtag) prior to the word that users want to be able to search on and group content by (Examples: #dogs or #agriculture). Users can follow a hashtag in the same manner they follow another Twitter user.

hi5—A social networking site designed to connect users with one another. hi5 includes "degrees of separation" (also seen in Friendster) and flash-powered chatrooms. http://hi5.com/

Hits—The number of times a resource (e.g., landing page, website, etc.) has been accessed via the Internet.

HootSuite—A Twitter client that allows users to manage multiple accounts, schedule tweets and measure activity. The services are focused on corporate users, typically monitoring multiple accounts, who are concerned with monitoring and shaping a company's brand via Twitter. http://hootsuite.com/

HTML—Hypertext markup language. A set of tags and rules for developing websites.

Hulu—A service that offers streaming content of TV shows and movies, supported through commercials. http://hulu.com/

iGoogle—Google's portal that allows users to customize their homepage by selecting different Google Gadgets (such as Calendar, Weather, News), which are then aggregated on the homepage. http://www.google.com/ig

Influencer—In the realm of social media, this is an individual who is able to persuade others to think or act in a certain manner based on user-generated content (e.g., comments on a blog, rating on a product, etc.). The best social influencers are users who are perceived to be authentic and trusted in the topics about which they are communicating.

Jing—Software that allows users to record their computer screen, mouse movements and voice for sharing and distribution via e-mail, instant messenger or over the web. http://www.jingproject.com

Keyword—A subject term, heading or description that is typically included in the HTML code of a website in a meta tag for search engines to index and crawl.

KickApps—Software-as-a-Service social media application that allows users to create their own online social networking communities based on unique areas of interest. http://www.kickapps.com/

Lifestreaming—An online aggregation of an individual's daily activities such as blog posts, social network updates, video and photo uploads.

Linkbaiting—Also known as link bait, the act of using enticing content on a user's website to attract other users. The term can refer to optimization for SEO, useful tools and/or specific content.

LinkedIn—Business-focused social networking site centered on professional (rather than social) connections among users. Users can "recommend" other users, search for users by industry functions and connect with current contacts. http://www.linkedin.com/

Link—Otherwise known as a hyperlink, this is a reference on a web page that points to some other place, either on the same page or site, or to an external content course. Whenever content is "clickable" this means it has been hyperlinked to additional content.

Mashup—A website, software tool or web service that combines two or more tools, gadgets or applications to create a single new application. Typically content for a mashup is sourced from a third party via a public interface or API, Web feeds and web services.

Meebo—A website for accessing multiple instant messaging platforms such as AOL Instant Messenger, Google Talk and Yahoo! Messenger from a single service. http://www.meebo.com/

Meta tag—An HTML tag, typically found in the header of a webpage that describes the content of the webpage. For example, the meta tag keyword lists all the keywords for the page that will be searched and indexed by search engines.

Metrics—Counts, ratios and key performance indicators that can be aggregated and segmented to analyze users' behavior on the web. Common metrics are the number of hits a webpage receives or the number of click-throughs from an advertisement to an advertiser's website.

Microblogging—A web service (such as Twitter) that allows subscribers to broadcast short messages (typically 140 characters) to other subscribers of the service. Microposts can be made on a website and/or distributed to a group of subscribers and can be read online or as an instant message to a mobile device.

Moblog—A blog that has been posted from a mobile device.

Movable Type—An online publishing platform created by Six Apart comprised of features such as multiple weblogs, standalone content pages, user and role management, customizable templates and categories for articles. http://www.movabletype.org/

MySpace—A social networking site owned by Fox Interactive Media. The site has been most popular amongst musicians for distributing their music and gaining fan support. http://www.myspace.com/

Navigation—The arrangement of menus, links and lists that allow a user to move among different segments of information and pages of a website.

NetVibes—A web portal (similar to iGoogle) that allows users to add built-in modules (gadgets or widgets) to their personal homepage such as an RSS feed reader, local weather forecasts, Flicker photos and more. http://www.netvibes.com/

News Aggregator—A website or software tool that allows news from multiple sources to be brought together (either automatically based on a keyword, subject or source, or manually) and displayed.

Newsgator—A software company primarily known for its family of RSS feed readers. Newsgator provides behind-the-firewall (a "private" network not accessible outside a company) social collaboration and media for businesses. http://www.newsgator.com/

Ning—A social networking service that enables users to build their own communities based on common interests and passions they wish to share online with one another. http://www.ning.com/

Online Newsroom—Also known as a pressroom, media room, press center or media center. Typically a part of a company's website that contains investor and analyst-focused news about the company. Typically the newsroom will include company press releases, announcements about quarterly earnings calls and community relations announcements.

Permalink—Also known as a permanent link. This is a static or permanent link to something, most typically to a specific blog or article, on a page that is constantly adding new content. Permalinks are used so that these stories can be linked from other pages or bookmarked in order to allow users to find them in the future.

Photobucket—A social networking website that allows image hosting, video hosting, slideshow creation and photo sharing by e-mail, instant message and mobile phone. http://photobucket.com/

Photosharing—Uploading, publishing and transferring of a user's photos online, allowing the user to share photos with other users both privately and publicly. This functionality is provided by photo-spe-cific websites such as Flickr, Picasa, Photobucket and social networking sites such as Facebook and MySpace.

Picasa—A software application provided by Google that allows both photo editing, organizing and photosharing. http://picasa.google.com/

Ping.fm—A social networking site that allows users to update their status, blogs and microblogs from one account to different social websites at once. http://ping.fm/

Podcast—Downloadable audio and video files that are released episodically.

Podcast Alley—A portal that provides an online directory for podcasts and podcasting information. http://www.podcastalley.com/

Podcasting—The act of creating and distributing a podcast.
Podosphere—The community or social network of podcasts.

Post—A comment, original article or thought that a user creates and uploads or "posts" to the Internet.

Profile—The collection of personal information users post about themselves that they can make available to the broader public or only to select users they "friend" (approve) on social networking sites.

Retweet (RT)—A reposting (or resending) of another Twitter user's post (displays on Twitter as "RT @ username").

RSS Feed—Known as Really Simple Syndication. This is an XML file that is used to publish frequently updated content such as blogs and news headlines in a standardized format for consumption by websites, e-mail and mobile phones.

Search—To actively look for a topic, piece of content or other type of information. Common search engines on the Internet today include Google, Yahoo! and Bing.

Search Engine Marketing (SEM)—A form of Internet marketing that seeks to promote websites by increasing their popularity and/or visibility in search engine result pages through monetary means such as paid placement, contextual advertising and paid inclusion.

Search Engine Optimization (SEO)—The process of using keywords and other code/content edits to websites in order to increase their popularity and/or visibility in search engine result pages.

Second Life—Massive multiplayer universe (MMU) set in a virtual 3D world, accessed via the Internet that allows its users (called Residents) to interact with each other through the use of avatars. Residents can socialize, create and trade virtual property and travel throughout the world, referred to as a grid. http://secondlife.com/

Sentiment Metrics—A social media monitoring company that measures a company's digital footprint with what customers are saying about the brand through blogs, discussion boards, press releases and news sites. http://www.sentimentmetrics.com/

Shutterfly—Internet-based social expression and personal publishing service that enables users to share, print and preserve their photos. http://www.shutterfly.com/

Skype—A social networking software that allows users to make free calls over the Internet to other Skype users. http://www.skype.com/

Slideshare—An Internet service for sharing presentations online. Users can upload, view and share presentation files with other users. http://www.slideshare.net/

Social Bookmarking—A method for users to share, organize, search and manage their bookmarks of web resources via the Internet.

Social Media—The collection of online conversations in which users share opinions, thoughts and information with one another via the Internet and mobile devices.

Social Media Policy—A set of guidelines shaped by an organization that outlines general principles surrounding how users should communicate online within the context of representing that organization or community.

Social Media Press Release—An interactive press release distributed via e-mail or social media vehicles such as podcasts, Skype phone numbers, Twitter posts and blogs. The social media press release centers on providing media with access to timely content in a variety of formats.

Social Mention—A social media search and analysis platform that aggregates user-generated content from across sites into a single stream of information. http://www.social-mention.com/

Social Networking—The grouping of individuals into specific groups and communities that interact with each other through social networking websites.

Spam—An unwanted e-mail, usually of a commercial nature and disseminated en masse. Most e-mail providers provide "spam" filters that aim to keep unwanted e-mail out of users' inboxes.

Squidoo—A community website that allows users to create pages (called lenses) for subjects of interest, thus becoming instant "experts" on a particular topic. http://www.squidoo.com/

Style Sheet—The cascading style sheet (CSS) is a master document used to describe the look and feel (font size, color, formatting, etc.) of a website.

Tag—A keyword or phrase used to categorize a piece of content. The collection of tags for a website can then be aggregated and displayed in a tag cloud (also called a word cloud).

Tag Cloud—A visual representation of user-generated tags with the popularity of the tag depicted by bolder, larger font than less popular tags.

Taxonomy—The classification of pages in a website into logical groupings used to create the site structure and navigation. Taxonomies are generally built for the purpose of simplifying the user's experience.

Technorati—An Internet search engine used for cataloguing and searching blogs. http://technorati.com/

Time-shifted Media—The Web 2.0 standard of offering content that can be consumed at a time of the user's choice, as opposed to when the publisher determines to provide it (e.g., YouTube videos and podcasts, can be viewed or listened to all the time, any time).

TinyURL—A web service that provides short aliases for long website URLs in order to make the URLs easier to remember and user friendly. http://www.tinyurl.com/

Trackback—Also referred to as linkback, this is a method for content creators to request notification when someone links to their content.

Tweet—A microblog posting on Twitter of up to 140 characters.

TweetBeep—An e-mail alert from Twitter to notify a user when another user mentions a username, product, company or keyword.

TweetDeck—A Twitter client that allows users to customize their Twitter experience by segmenting users into groups and conversations for easier sending and receiving of tweets. http://www.tweetdeck.com

Tweetie—Twitter client that has both a mobile version for the iPhone and iPod Touch and a desktop version for Mac OS X. Tweetie allows multiple Twitter accounts to be managed from an iPhone or iPod Touch. http://www.tweetie.com/

TwitPic—Website that allows users to post a photo to Twitter. TwitPic is often used by citizen journalists to upload and distribute photos in real time as an event is taking place. http://twitpic.com/

TwitVid—A Twitter client that allows users to post video to Twitter. http://twitvid.com/

Twitter—A social networking and microblogging service that enables users to send and receive messages (called Tweets) to and from other Twitter users. Message must be no longer than 140 characters in length. http://twitter.com/

TwitterBerry—A mobile Twitter client specific to BlackBerry mobile devices that allows users to access Twitter from a BlackBerry Twitter application.

Twitter Client—Any software application designed to create ease of use when using Twitter (e.g., TwitPic, which lets users share photos on Twitter via an API, TwitVid, which enables video sharing, or TweetDeck, which helps users to manage followers, content and tracking).

Twittersphere—The universe of Twitter users and their accounts.

TypePad—A hosted blogging service from the company Six Apart designed for bloggers. http://www.typepad.com/

UberTwitter—An advanced Twitter client developed especially for BlackBerry phones. UberTwitter provides features such as one-touch re-tweeting (RT), GPS integration and quick photo upload using MyPict. http://www.ubertwitter.com/

URL—The address of a webpage on the Internet (Example: http://www.google.com is Google's URL).

URL Shortening—A service that translates long URLs into abbreviated alternatives (e.g., services such as TinyURL, bit.ly, or owl.ly through HootSuite).

User-Generated Content—Also known as consumer-generated media or user-created content. Media content that is produced by end users, as opposed to traditional media producers and publishers, such as licensed broadcasters and production companies.

Viddler—An Internet platform that enables users to upload videos, record videos directly from a webcam, post comments and tags at specific points in the video and share videos via RSS and iTunes. http://www.viddler.com/

Videosharing—The uploading and distribution of videos via the Internet. Multiple videosharing services exist such as Viddler, Vimeo and YouTube.

Vimeo—An Internet platform aimed at enabling users with video content to share, collaborate and distribute video assets. http://www.vimeo.com/

Viral—A video, image or text spread by "word of mouth" on the Internet or by e-mail with the goal of immediate, mass attention and buzz.

Vlog—Video blog.

Voice Over Internet Protocol (VOIP)—The delivery of voice communication over the Internet.

Web 2.0—The second generation of web development defined by the focus on user communication and interactions. The term has been widely attributed to Tim O'Reilly of the O'Reilly Media Group.

Web log—Also known as blog. An online diary used to share content (text, video, photos, etc.) with users via the Internet. It is frequently updated by a blogger (generally via 500- to 1,100-word text updates) and can range from topics about the user's personal life and experience to product reviews, industry analysis and more.

Webinar—A conference call, live presentation or recorded presentation delivered over the Internet. Webinars can be accompanied by a live phone call or a recorded audio track.

Widget—A small portion of code, program or application that can be embedded into a third-party website. Users download the widget to a reader or desktop, and the content will be brought to them via a feed through the widget (Example: local weather, stock ticker, movie showtimes and more can be packaged as widgets).

Wiffiti—An Internet service that publishes real-time messages to large screens (e.g., users type their messages via a mobile device or web-based application, and the message appears on an associated large or jumbo screen at event sites). http://wiffiti.com/

Wiki—A website that allows the creation and editing of web content via a web browser using a simple text editor. This makes content easy to edit or update by any non-technical user.

Wikifarms—A server or an array of servers that offers users tools to simplify the creation and development of individual or independent wikis.

Wikipedia—Online content encyclopedia created through the collaborative efforts of a community of users known as Wikipedians. Anyone registered for Wikipedia can create an article for publication. http://wikipedia.org/

Word-of-mouth marketing (WOMM)—The passing of information from one user to another. Social media and the Internet have caused markets to take a vested interest in leveraging WOMM to optimize results.

XML—eXtensible Markup Language. An open standard for structuring information such as RSS feeds. XML is the recommended standard for creating formats and sharing data on the Internet.

YouTube—Social networking website where users can upload and share videos. http://www.youtube.com

SURVIVAL KIT

Links You Can Use

ONLINE NEWSROOM EXAMPLES

Accenture
http://newsroom.accenture.com/index.cfm

Allstate Insurance
http://www.allstatenewsroom.com/

American Civil Liberties Union
http://www.aclu.org/news

American Red Cross
http://newsroom.redcross.org/

Amway
http://www.amwayglobalnews.com/pr/awg/default.aspx

BASF Ventures
http://www.basf.com/group/corporate/en_GB/content/news-and-media-relations/press-releases

Baxter
http://www.baxter.com/about_baxter/press_room/index.html?WT.svl=urlforwarding

British Petroleum
http://www.bp.com/productlanding.do?categoryId=120&contentId=7047744

Boeing
http://boeing.mediaroom.com/

The California Endowment
http://tcenews.calendow.org/pr/tce/default.aspx

Carmax
http://media.carmax.com/pr/carmax/default.aspx

Centers for Disease Control
http://www.cdc.gov/media/

Chevron
http://www.chevron.com/

Children's Hospital, Boston
http://www.childrenshospital.org/newsroom

Cisco Systems
http://newsroom.cisco.com/

Crayola
http://www.crayola.com/mediacenter/

Dell
http://content.dell.com/us/en/corp/about-dell-press-room.aspx

Ford Motor Company
http://media.ford.com/

Genentech
http://www.gene.com/gene/news/index.jsp

Google
http://www.google.com/press/index.html

Hewlett Packard
http://www.hp.com/hpinfo/newsroom/

Intel
http://www.intel.com/capital/news/index.htm

Microsoft
http://www.microsoft.com/presspass/default.mspx

Nestle
http://www.nestle.com/MediaCenter/MediaCenter.htm

The Northwest Area Foundation
http://www.nwaf.org/Content/News

National Arbitration Forum
http://www.adrforum.com/main.aspx?itemID=237&hideBar=False&navID
=6&news=3

Pfizer
http://www.pfizer.com/news/

Proctor & Gamble
http://www.pg.com/news/index.shtml

Rosetta Stone
http://pr.rosettastone.com/

Schubert Communications
http://newsroom.schubert.com/

Shift Communications
http://www.shiftcomm.com/newsroom/

Smith & Hawken
http://pressroom.smithandhawken.com/pr/shnews/pressroom-home.aspx

Sun Microsystems
http://www.sun.com/aboutsun/media/index.jsp

Target
http://pressroom.target.com/pr/news/news.
aspx?ref=nav%5Ffooter%5Fnews

TEKgroup International
http://newsroom.tekgroup.com/

Toshiba
http://www.toshiba.com/tai/news/news.jsp

Toyota
http://pressroom.toyota.com/pr/tms/

Valero
http://www.valero.com/newsroom/Pages/Home.aspx

Walgreens
http://news.walgreens.com/

Whole Foods Market
http://wholefoodsmarket.com/pressroom/

Walmart
http://walmartstores.com/FactsNews/

World Wildlife Federation
http://www.worldwildlife.org/who/media/index.html?linklocation=footers
itemap

Xiotech
http://www.xiotech.com/About_Press_Press-Analyst-Center.aspx

ONLINE NEWSROOM VENDORS

---

iPressroom
http://www.ipressroom.com/pr/corporate/default.aspx

News Cactus
http://www.newscactus.com/

TEKgroup International
http://www.tekgroup.com/products/#TEKmedia

Vocus Online Newsroom
http://www.vocus.com/content/prnewsroom.asp

Xigla Software
http://www.xigla.com/absolutenm/features.htm

TOOLS FOR MANAGING CONTENT AND TRACKING

AIM Share
Enables users to post and share content onto their AOL Instant Messenger
Account.
http://share.aim.com/share/

Bebo
Enables users to share content on their Bebo social networking account.
http://www.bebo.com

BlinkList
Allows users to save links on their BlinkList account for future viewing,
sharing and running searches for similar content.
http://www.blinklist.com

Blogger
Enables users to share content on their own Google blog.
http://www.blogger.com

Blogmarks
Enables users to share and categorize content on their Blogmarks social
bookmarking account.
http://blogmarks.net

BuzzUp!
Enables users to upload content to the BuzzUp! tech blog.
http://buzzup.com/us/

Care2
Enables users to upload information to their Care2 accounts, an eco-cen-
tered lifestyle website.
http://www.care2.com/

Current
Uploads blog posts or articles to user's current website.
http://current.com/

Delicious
Social bookmarking services; adds blog to users' list of online bookmarks.
http://delicious.com

Digg
Uploads blog posts to digg.com to be voted upon by Internet users.
http://www.digg.com

Diigo
Enables users to bookmark and share content on their Diigo toolbar and/or account.
http://www.diigo.com

Facebook
Allows users to share content on their Facebook pages.
http://www.facebook.com

Fark
Enables users to post, comment and vote on blog content on fark.com.
http://www.fark.com

Faves
Enables users to add content to their faves social bookmarking account.
http://faves.com/home

Flickr
Allows users to post content on Flickr pages.
http://www.flickr.com

FriendFeed
Allows users to upload content to their FriendFeed to share with other FriendFeed users.
http://friendfeed.com/

G Bookmarks
Adds content to users' Google bookmark page.
http://www.google.com/bookmarks/?ctz=300

Kirtsy
Enables users to share various articles and blogs covering a broad range of information.
http://www.kirtsy.com

Lifestrea.ms
A web-based e-mail client, allowing users to send content to their Lifestream.
http://lifestrea.ms/

LinkedIn
Enables users to share blog or news content on their Linkedin account.
http://www.linkedin.com

Livejournal
Posts and shares content onto users' Livejournal blog pages.
http://www.livejournal.com/

Mixx
Allows users to share information found on their Mixx account.
http://www.mixx.com

Mister Wong
Social bookmarking service, allowing users to bookmark blog or news content.
http://www.mister-wong.com/

MySpace
Enables users to add content to their MySpace page.
http://www.myspace.com

Newsvine
Allows user to post content as a part of a new story on their open source Newsvine account.
http://www.newsvine.com

Ping
Enables users to upload content to multiple social networking sites at once.
http://ping.fm/

Posterous
Enables users to upload any form of content via e-mail.
http://posterous.com/

Propeller
Enables users to share and vote upon news stories.
http://www.propeller.com/

Reddit
Enables users to post content on their Reddit account to be voted on.
http://www.reddit.com

ShareThis
Adds newsroom articles or blog posts to users' ShareThis account, an
account that stores and shares one's most visited websites from multiple
devices.
http://sharethis.com/#STS=g2yzs5fg.g0i

Slashdot
Allows users to post and share content to their Slashdot technology-
oriented blog.
http://slashdot.org

Simpy
Enables users to add, save, comment and tag content within the simpy
social bookmarking service.
http://www.simpy.com

Stumbleupon
Enables users to add a blog to the Stumbleupon application so that similar
blogs can be brought to their attention.
http://www.stumbleupon.com

Technorati
Enables users to upload content to their technorati.com blog.
www.technorati.com

Trendrr
Allows users to track content keywords on each blog.
http://www.trendrr.com/

Tumblr
Allows users to post content on their Tumblelog mini-blog.
http://www.tumblr.com

Twackle
Enables users to post content on their Twackle, a sports-oriented Twitter
account.
http://www.twackle.com

Twine
Enables users to add content to their Twine information page.
http://www.twine.com

TypePad
Enables users to share information found on their TypePad run blog.
http://www.typepad.com/

Upcoming
Allows users to post content from the blog on their "Upcoming events
page."
http://upcoming.yahoo.com/

Windows Live
Enables users to make the news page a "shared favorite" on their Windows
Live or Hotmail account.
http://www.hotmail.com

WordPress
Enables users to add content to their WordPress blogs.
http://wordpress.org/

Xanga
Enables users to post content on their xanga blog.
http://www.xanga.com

Yahoo Bookmarks
Enables users to save and organize content in their Yahoo Bookmark account.
http://bookmarks.yahoo.com/

SOCIAL MEDIA POLICY EXAMPLES

123 Social Media
http://123socialmedia.com/2009/01/23/social-media-policy-examples/
Includes policy examples from:
Associated Press Social Media Policy
BBC – Editorial Guidelines, personal use of Social Networking
Blog Council – Disclosure Policy
Chartered Institute of Public Relations (CIPR) Social Media Guidelines
CIPR – Social Media Guidelines for Consultation
CISCO Internet Postings Policy
CivilService – Code for Online Participation
Dow Jones Social Media Interaction Policy
ESPN Employee Social Media Policy
ESPN Talent / Anchor Social Media Policy
Gartner Web Participation Policy
General Motors Blogging Policy
Government Policy
Greteman Group (Marketing Agency)
Harvard Law School – Terms & Policy
HP Code of Conduct
IBM Social Computing Guidelines
Intel – Social Media Guidelines
Kodak Social Media Policy/Marketing Book
Opera Employee Blogging Policies
Porter Novelli
Sun Guidelines on Public Disclosure
US Air Force Social Media Policy (with flow chart)
US Navy – Web 2.0 – Utilizing New Web Tools
Wall Street Journal
Wells Fargo Community Guidelines

Candid CIO
http://candidcio.com/2009/08/12/social-media-policy-and-employee-guidance/

Dave Fleet
http://davefleet.com/2009/05/social-media-policies-company-internal-policies/

Laurel Papworth
http://www.laurelpapworth.com
Includes policy examples from:
About.com generic ones
http://humanresources.about.com/od/policysamplesb/a/blogging_policy.htm
BBC
http://www.bbc.co.uk/guidelines/editorialguidelines/advice/personalweb/blogging.shtml
The Blogging Church
http://www.leaveitbehind.com/home/2005/04/fellowship_chur.html
Canadian Broadcasting Corporation
http://www.insidethecbc.com/bloggingrules
Chartered Institute of Public Relations Social Media Guidelines
http://www.cipr.co.uk/socialmedia/
Cisco
http://blogs.cisco.com/news/comments/ciscos_internet_postings_policy/
The City of Seattle
http://www.seattle.gov/pan/SocialMediaPolicy.htm
Dell's Online Communication Policy http://www.dell.com/content/topics/global.aspx/policy/en/policy?c=us&l=en&s=corp&~section=019
Electronic Frontier Foundation How to Blog Safely about Work
http://www.eff.org/wp/blog-safely
Feedster's Corporate Blogging Policy
http://feedster.blogs.com/corporate/2005/03/corporate_blogg.html
Gartner's Public Web Participation Guidelines
http://blogs.gartner.com/gartner-public-web-participation-guidelines/
General Motors Blogging Policies
http://fastlane.gmblogs.com/about.html
Greteman Group Blog Social Media Policy http://gretemangroup.com/blog/index.php/2009/01/social-media-policy/
Harvard Law School Blogs Terms of Use
http://blogs.law.harvard.edu/terms-of-use/
Hewlett Packard Blogging Code of Conduct
http://www.hp.com/hpinfo/blogs/codeofconduct.html

Hill and Knowlton's Public Relations Pledge for Bloggers
http://armadgeddon.blogspot.com/2007/09/h-pledge-for-bloggers.html

IBM's Social Computing Guidelines
http://www.ibm.com/blogs/zz/en/guidelines.html

Intel Social Media Guidelines
http://www.intel.com/sites/sitewide/en_US/social-media.htm

IOC Olympic Athletes Blogging Policy http://multimedia.olympic.org/pdf/
en_report_1296.pdf

LiveWorld Social Media Content Guidelines http://socialvoice.liveworld.
com/blog-entry/Bryan-Persons-Blog/Creating-Social-Media/1100000608

Opera
http://my.opera.com/community/blogs/corp-policy/

Plaxo's Communication (Blogging) Policies http://blog.plaxoed.
com/2005/03/29/plaxos-communication-policy/

Sun Guidelines on Public Discourse
http://www.sun.com/communities/guidelines.jsp
http://www.sun.com/aboutsun/media/blogs/BloggingGuidelines.pdf

Thomas Nelson Blogging Policy
http://michaelhyatt.blogs.com/workingsmart/2005/03/corporate_blogg_1.
html

Walker Art Center
http://newmedia.walkerart.org/nmiwiki/pmwiki.php/Main/WalkerBlog
Guidelines

Yahoo's Personal Blog Guidelines for Staff
http://jeremy.zawodny.com/yahoo/yahoo-blog-guidelines.pdf

Social Media Governance
http://socialmediagovernance.com/policies.php
Include policy examples from:
About.com
American Red Cross
Australian Public Service Commission
Baker & Daniels
BBC
BBYO
Bread for the World
BT

Canadian Broadcasting Corporation (CBC)
Chartered Institute of Public Relations (CIPR)
Children's Hospital Los Angeles
Cisco
City of Hampton
City of Seattle
Cleveland Clinic
Dell
DePaul University
Easter Seals
Electronic Frontier Foundation
ESPN
eWay Direct
Fairfax County, VA
FedEx
Feedster
Fellowship Church
FINRA
Fudder Netiquette
Gartner
General Services Administration (GSA)
GM
Greteman Group
Harvard Law School
Headset Brothers
Hill and Knowlton
HP
IBM
InQbation
Intel
International Federation of Red Cross and Red Crescent Societies (IFRC)
International Olympic Committee (IOC)
Iowa Hospital Association
Jaffe
Judith Lindeau
Kaiser Permanente
Kodak Social Media Tips
Le Bonheur Children's Medical Center
LiveWorld
Mayo Clinic

Media Law Resource Center
Microsoft
Missouri Department of Transportation
National Public Radio (NPR)
New Zealand State Services Commission
Oce
Opera
Plaxo
Porter Novelli
Powerhouse Museum
PR-Squared
Razorfish
Rhetorica
RightNow
Roanoke County
Roanoke Times
Robert Scoble
SAP
Sentara Social Media Policy
Shift Communications
Smithsonian Institution
Social Media Business Council
SpareBank
State of Delaware
Sun Microsystems
Telstra
The University of Texas MD Anderson Cancer Center
The Well
Thomas Nelson
U.K. Civil Service
U.S. Air Force
U.S. Army Corps of Engineers
U.S. Coast Guard
U.S. Environmental Protection Agency (EPA)
U.S. Federal Trade Commission (FTC)
U.S. General Services Administration
U.S. Navy
Unic
University of Maryland Medical Center
Wake County, NC

Walmart
Walker Art Center
Washington Post (via PaidContent.org)
Webtrends
Wells Fargo
Workplace Fairness
Yahoo!

SAMPLE SOCIAL MEDIA PRESS RELEASES

Accenture
http://newsroom.accenture.com/article_display.cfm?article_id=4913

American Red Cross
http://www.redcross.org/portal/site/en/menuitem.94aae335470e233f6cf91
1df43181aa0/?vgnextoid=2ed3b2423d265210VgnVCM10000089f0870aRC
RD

Barrick Gold
http://www.barrick.com/News/PressReleases/PressReleaseDetails/2009/
BarrickGoldCorporationAppealsCourtRemandsDecisiontoDistrictCour-
tonCortezHillsProject1121331/default.aspx

Chevron
http://investor.chevron.com/phoenix.zhtml?c=130102&p=irol-
newsArticle&ID=1362266&highlight=

General Motors
http://media.gm.com/content/media/us/en/news/news_detail.html/con-
tent/Pages/news/us/en/2009/Dec/1208_reuss_docherty

GNC
http://gnc.mediaroom.com/index.php?s=43&item=213

Home Depot
http://phx.corporate-ir.net/phoenix.zhtml?c=63646&p=RssLanding&cat=n
ews&id=1362510

Microsoft
http://www.microsoft.com/presspass/press/2009/dec09/12-08MSNOn-lineLifestylePR.mspx

Nissan
http://www.nissan-global.com/EN/NEWS/2009/_STORY/091201-01-e.html

Peace Corps
http://www.peacecorps.gov/index.cfm?shell=resources.media.press.view&news_id=1513

Saks Fifth Avenue
http://phx.corporate-ir.net/phoenix.zhtml?c=110111&p=irol-newsArticle&ID=1361652&highlight=

Shift Communications
http://www.socialmedianews.ca/pdfs/SocialMediaNewsReleaseTemplate.pdf

Swatch Group
http://www.swatchgroup.com/en/services/archive/2009/le_cio_et_le_swatch_group_sa_signent_un_partenariat_a_long_terme

Time Warner
http://www.timewarner.com/corp/newsroom/pr/0,20812,1945499,00.html

Verizon
http://investor.verizon.com/news/view.aspx?NewsID=1025

World Wildlife Federation
http://www.worldwildlife.org/who/media/press/2009/WWFPresitem14528.html

SOCIAL MEDIA PRESS RELEASE "HOW-TO" SITES

http://www.socialmedianews.ca/index.php?option=com_weblinks&view=category&id=51%3Aonline-newsrooms&Itemid=124

http://www.future-works.com/about/agency_news/files/How%20To%20Write%20SMPRs%20by%20Brian%20Solis.pdf

SAMPLE ANNUAL REPORTS

From Nexxar
http://www.nexxar.com/marketresearch/usadowjones30.html
List of annual reports includes:
AT&T
Chevron
Cisco Systems
Disney
General Electric
Home Depot
IBM
Intel
Merck &Co
Microsoft
Procter and Gamble
Verizon
Walmart

SAMPLE SOCIAL MEDIA CORPORATE INVESTOR RELATIONS SITES

Amazon
http://phx.corporate-ir.net/phoenix.zhtml?p=irol-irhome&c=97664

Apple
http://phx.corporate-ir.net/phoenix.zhtml?c=107357&p=irol-index

Barrick Gold
http://www.barrick.com/Investors/default.aspx

Chevron
http://investor.chevron.com/phoenix.zhtml?c=130102&p=irol-irhome

Cisco Systems
http://investor.cisco.com/

CitiGroup
http://www.citibank.com/citi/fin/

Disney
http://corporate.disney.go.com/investors/index.html

Ford
http://www.ford.com/about-ford/investor-relations

General Electric
http://www.ge.com/investors/index.html

General Motors
http://www.gm.com/corporate/investor_information/

Home Depot
http://ir.homedepot.com/phoenix.zhtml?c=63646&p=irol-IRHome

IBM
http://www.ibm.com/investor/?cm_re=wspace-_-horznav-_-learn

Intel
http://www.intc.com/

Merck &Co
http://www.merck.com/investors/home.html

Microsoft
http://www.microsoft.com/msft/default.mspx

Procter and Gamble
http://www.pg.com/investors/sectionmain.shtml
Saks Fifth Avenue
http://phx.corporate-ir.net/phoenix.zhtml?c=110111&p=irol-irhome

Toyota
http://www.toyota.co.jp/en/ir/index.html

Time Warner
http://ir.timewarner.com/phoenix.zhtml?c=70972&p=irol-irhome

Verizon
http://investor.verizon.com/

Virgin Media
http://investors.virginmedia.com/phoenix.zhtml?c=135485&p=irol-irhome

Walgreens
http://investor.walgreens.com/

Walmart
http://investors.walmartstores.com/phoenix.zhtml?c=112761&p=irol-irhome

INTRODUCING...

The Social Media Survival Guide Series

Just as organizations and individuals are eager to embrace the opportunity, they are hesitant to take on additional risk, leaving many to fall behind the competition in the wake of uncertainty. **The Social Media Survival Guide** and its companion titles are designed to make social media accessible, tactical and easy to use right away. **The Survival Guide** series will help you to market successfully within this space, maintain a competitive edge and boost results—from increasing sales, to landing the job, to winning elections.

  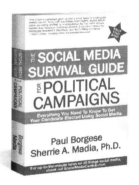

The Social Media Survival Guide (Spanish-language edition)
June 2010

The Online Job Search Survival Guide: Everything You Need to Know to Use Social Networking to Land a Job Now
Spring 2010

The Social Media Survival Guide for Political Campaigns: Everything You Need to Know to Get Your Candidate Elected Using Social Media
Summer 2010

Pre-order at SocialMediaSurvivalGuide.com

Manufactured By: RR Donnelley
                     Breinigsville, PA USA
                     October, 2010